Cambridge Elements ☰

Elements in New Religious Movements
edited by
James R. Lewis
Wuhan University
Rebecca Moore
San Diego State University

D0841198

L. RON HUBBARD AND SCIENTOLOGY STUDIES

Donald A. Westbrook
San Jose State University

CAMBRIDGE
UNIVERSITY PRESS

CAMBRIDGE
UNIVERSITY PRESS

University Printing House, Cambridge CB2 8BS, United Kingdom

One Liberty Plaza, 20th Floor, New York, NY 10006, USA

477 Williamstown Road, Port Melbourne, VIC 3207, Australia

314–321, 3rd Floor, Plot 3, Splendor Forum, Jasola District Centre, New Delhi – 110025, India

103 Penang Road, #05–06/07, Visioncrest Commercial, Singapore 238467

Cambridge University Press is part of the University of Cambridge.

It furthers the University's mission by disseminating knowledge in the pursuit of education, learning, and research at the highest international levels of excellence.

www.cambridge.org
Information on this title: www.cambridge.org/9781009014557
DOI: 10.1017/9781009032001

First published 2022

A catalogue record for this publication is available from the British Library.

ISBN 978-1-009-01455-7 Paperback
ISSN 2635-232X (online)
ISSN 2635-2311 (print)

Cambridge University Press has no responsibility for the persistence or accuracy of URLs for external or third-party internet websites referred to in this publication and does not guarantee that any content on such websites is, or will remain, accurate or appropriate.

L. Ron Hubbard and Scientology Studies

Elements in New Religious Movements

DOI: 10.1017/9781009032001
First published online: June 2022

Donald A. Westbrook
San Jose State University

Author for correspondence: Donald A. Westbrook, donald.westbrook@sjsu.edu

Abstract: This Element surveys the history and practice of Scientology studies over the past sixty years and offers resources for scholars and students moving forward. Section 1 reviews the history of academic research on the subject from 1958 to the present day. Section 2 draws on the author's fieldwork with the Church of Scientology to illuminate how founder L. Ron Hubbard (1911–86) is viewed among contemporary members. Section 3 considers Hubbard's influence and legacy in terms of the church sites and institutions that exist today in connection with the soteriological "Bridge to Total Freedom." Section 4 introduces English-language archival resources and their strengths. Section 5 proposes some open areas for Scientology researchers. Finally, glossaries of terms and appendices are included with major dates in Hubbard's life and Scientology research and bibliographical information for major archival collections in North America.

Keywords: L. Ron Hubbard, Scientology studies, new religious movements, Church of Scientology, Scientologists

ISBNs: 9781009014557 (PB), 9781009032001 (OC)
ISSNs: 2635-232X (online), 2635-2311 (print)

Contents

Introduction

For many, the Church of Scientology is associated with a science fiction (SF) writer named L. Ron Hubbard (1911–86), celebrity adherents, esoteric scriptures, allegations of abuse, claims of brainwashing and cult status, a pay-as-you-go theology, an episode on the American TV show *South Park*, and a plethora of anti-Scientology books and documentaries (especially over the past decade). In a 2008 Gallup poll (Jones 2008), 52 percent of Americans surveyed had a "total negative" view of Scientologists. This was the highest of all religious groups surveyed, ahead of both Muslims and atheists, respectively. Only 7 percent of Gallup respondents reported a "total positive" view of Scientology, with 37 percent indicating that they were "neutral" on the topic.

This perception in popular culture is to a large extent a reflection of the literature about the Church of Scientology that has influenced the popular imagination since the 1950s. As the historian J. Gordon Melton put it more than twenty years ago, "Overwhelmingly, books on Scientology have been either publications by the church expounding and defending its position or attacks by its critics" (2000: 79). In more recent years, the academic scene at least has begun to change dramatically, resulting in what James R. Lewis referred to as a "small tsunami of new scholarship" (Lewis & Hellesøy 2017: 2). Massimo Introvigne has used the expression "Scientology studies 2.0" (2017a, 2018a, 2020; Westbrook 2020) to describe the more substantive approaches to the subject that are now emerging on the scholarly landscape.

This Element offers an overview of the history of Scientology studies, a subject that has received increased attention among scholars of new religious movements (NRMs) in particular (see, e.g., Dericquebourg 2017a; Religious Studies Podcast 2018; Doherty 2019; Gregg & Thomas 2019; Westbrook, 2019: 6, 204–06; Cusack 2020; Thomas 2020). In presenting the state of this field, I address problems of access and the place of academics in the Scientological imagination. I also turn to possible productive paths forward for would-be researchers of L. Ron Hubbard, Dianetics, and Scientology. This short work cannot and does not address all of the controversies associated with Hubbard and the church (see, e.g., Reitman 2011; Rathbun 2013; Wright 2013; Miller 2014), but rather is intended to help researchers navigate an academic subfield that continues to grow and develop in sophistication. Indeed, I have written this Element with graduate students and scholars primarily in mind, particularly those with a background in religious studies or a related interdisciplinary field such as history, sociology, or popular culture, and hope that any reader with an academic interest in Scientology will find it useful.

Section 1 surveys the history of academic research and also introduces some of the terminological issues that confront researchers of the subject. Section 2 is more ethnographic, drawing on my fieldwork with the Church of Scientology before turning attention to how Hubbard is perceived among Scientologists. Section 3 makes the case that one way to examine Hubbard's influence and legacy, on an everyday and experiential level among the faithful, is through the church sites and institutions he created and the path to spiritual freedom he created in the "Bridge to Total Freedom." Section 4 takes a pragmatic turn and introduces the variety of archival resources available, especially in the United States, to researchers. Section 5 concludes with areas that remain open for scholarly analysis. Glossaries of terms and acronyms provide some of the needed vocabulary for Scientology research. Appendix A includes major dates in the life of L. Ron Hubbard, Scientology history, and Scientology research. It notes issues of controversy that have occurred in the life of the church. Appendix B lists notable archival collections along with links to finding aids and further information.

1 Scientology Studies: Theory and Practice

The origins of Scientology studies – if by this we primarily mean, as I do, *academic* attention as opposed to journalistic or popular coverage – might be traced to a 1958 interview that L. Ron Hubbard granted to J. Stillson Judah, an NRM researcher and librarian from the Graduate Theological Union in Berkeley. Judah – who later became a well-known scholar of the Hare Krishna (ISKCON) movement and interviewed its leader as well (Judah 1975) – met Hubbard in his Washington, DC, office for an audio-recorded conversation that has been transcribed and published by the Church of Scientology (Hubbard 2012a: 87–91). Topics ranged from Hubbard's educational background to the origins of Scientology and, even earlier, the emergence of Dianetics, the mental health precursor to Scientology promulgated in the 1950 book *Dianetics: The Modern Science of Mental Health*. Dianetics became a national phenomenon in 1950 and its popular success laid the groundwork for the movement's more spiritual direction as Hubbard pursued the "religion angle," as he wrote to his secretary in 1953 ahead of incorporating the first churches of Scientology (Urban 2011: 65–68; Westbrook 2019: 83–85). Not everyone in the Dianetics movement welcomed this development, however, since it deviated from Hubbard's original scientific intentions (Winter 1951) and the work of the Hubbard Dianetic Research Foundation (Ibanez et al. 1951; Sterling 1952; Fox, Davis & Lebovits 1959; van Vogt 1964; O'Brien 1966).

Although the Church of Scientology was firmly in place by 1954, the first major academic study of Scientology was not produced until 1976 with Roy Wallis's seminal *The Road to Total Freedom: A Sociological Analysis of Scientology*. Based on interviews and fieldwork, some of it covert, Wallis examined the transition from the "epistemological individualism" of the 1950s Dianetics movement to the "epistemological authoritarianism" of the far more centralized Scientology churches (Wallis 1976/77: 14–18, 1975). One perception among outsiders, academics included, is that research and investigation of Scientology carry the risk of legal or even extralegal retaliation (see, e.g., Dallam 2011; Lord 2019). As a case study of this phenomenon, Wallis reported harassment at his university ahead of the publication of *The Road to Total Freedom*. He provided an advance copy of his work to church officials, incorporated numerous corrections, and even included a critical response authored by the Scientologist and sociologist J. L. Simmons (Wallis 1976/77: 265–69) in the final product. These difficulties may have deterred other researchers from this period, but one can find other publications in the intervening years (e.g., Bainbridge & Stark 1980) in evidence of ongoing academic research. The next major work on Scientology – and one that has too often been neglected in the literature, perhaps because the title does not adequately reveal its content – was the anthropologist Harriet Whitehead's *Renunciation and Reformulation: A Study of Conversion in an American Sect* (Whitehead 1987). Whitehead put forward a detailed account of auditing (i.e., mental/spiritual counseling), including features of Hubbard's electro-psychometer (E-Meter), based on fieldwork she conducted in Los Angeles among Scientologists for her dissertation at the University of Chicago entitled "What Does Scientology Auditing Do?" (Whitehead 1975). Whitehead in the United States, much like Wallis in the United Kingdom, relied largely on undercover or covert methods, which were more common and acceptable in the 1970s and predate the standards for consent now required by institutional review boards (IRBs).

In 1985 Roland Chagnon published a study of Scientologists in Canada, *La Scientologie: une nouvelle religion de la puissance* (*Scientology: A New Religion of Power*), that modeled the possibility of a more productive and cooperative relationship between a scholar and the church (Chagnon 1985). Another international work of note, and one that likewise received support from Scientologists, was Dorthe Refslund Christensen's 1999 dissertation at the University of Aarhus, "Rethinking Scientology: Cognition and Representation in Religion, Therapy, and Soteriology" (Christensen 1999). Christensen's research – which has been reproduced in articles and book chapters over the years (e.g., Christensen 2005, 2009, 2017) – offers an in-depth analysis of the transition from Dianetics (therapy) to Scientology (religion) based on

Hubbard's vast writings about auditing (especially the "Technical Bulletins") that are now counted as scripture in the church. However, not all researchers from the 1980s and 1990s achieved this level of camaraderie with the Scientologists they sought to study. One example is Stephen A. Kent, a sociologist at the University of Alberta, who has produced a sizable body of work on Scientology (see, e.g., Kent 1999) along with an impressive archive on alternative beliefs and religions. Kent and his colleague Susan Raine also edited the interdisciplinary volume *Scientology in Popular Culture: Influences and Struggles for Legitimacy* (Kent & Raine 2017). Kent's criticisms of Scientology have led to tensions with the church – which labeled him a "false expert" on one of its websites (STAND League 2019) – and also to disagreements with other scholars of new religions, such as J. Gordon Melton (1999) and James R. Lewis (1999).

Melton, a professor at Baylor University, is a senior and foundational figure in the study of NRMs. He is yet another example of a scholar who has maintained congenial relations with the Church of Scientology, dating to a 1964 visit to a branch in Chicago (Melton 2017: 11). Since then he has produced several important contributions to Scientology studies, such as his work on the Sea Organization (Sea Org), the church's priesthood and senior administrators (Melton 2018), and the introductory volume *The Church of Scientology* (Melton 2000). James R. Lewis, currently at Wuhan University, is another monumental presence in the field, having produced numerous works, including two edited volumes (Lewis 2009; Lewis & Hellesøy 2017) and special issues of *Alternative Spirituality and Religion Review* (2015) and *Numen* (2016) devoted to Scientology. In recent years Lewis and some of his graduate students in Norway, when he taught at the University of Tromsø, shifted attention away from the Church of Scientology and toward independent Scientologists who disaffiliate from the church yet remain committed to their own interpretations of Hubbard's philosophy and practices (Lewis 2013; Hellesøy 2015). This new approach has received attention from others, for example, Reza Aslan's CNN television show *Believer*, which featured a 2017 episode on Scientology reform groups (Introvigne 2017b), and Aled Thomas's dissertation at the Open University, "Auditing in Contemporary Scientologies: The Self, Authenticity, and Material Culture" (Thomas 2019).

The second decade of the twenty-first century also witnessed the production of four monographs. The first came with historian Hugh B. Urban's *The Church of Scientology: A History of a New Religion*, a sweeping account of L. Ron Hubbard and his creations from the 1950s to the present that was produced with cooperation from ex-members, critics, and independent Scientologists (Urban 2011). Urban has continued to publish on Scientology, including impressive articles on the connections between Hubbard, Gnosticism, religious secrecy, and Western esotericism (Urban 2012, 2017, 2019). The second came from Aldo Natale Terrin, a Catholic priest and theologian whose *Scientology: Libertà e immortalità* (*Scientology: Freedom and Immortality*) outlined the beliefs and practices of the church (Terrin 2017a). The Italian scholar included phenomenological and empathetic perspectives and compared Hubbard's creations with other traditions, such as Buddhism, Hinduism, New Thought, Theosophy, and especially Gnosticism (see also Terrin 2017b). The third monograph was my own *Among the Scientologists: History, Theology, and Praxis* (Westbrook 2019), based on fieldwork and interviews conducted with church members in the United States for PhD research at Claremont Graduate University. I have also published work in recent years on Scientology's "pilgrimage" sites (Westbrook 2016), intellectual history (Westbrook 2017b), evolving public relations (PR) strategies (Westbrook 2018), Gnosticism (Westbrook & Lewis 2019), and systematic theology (Westbrook 2015), including features of its antipsychiatric theology (Westbrook 2017c). The fourth and most recent monograph is Aled Thomas's *Free Zone Scientology: Contesting the Boundaries of a New Religion*, based on his interviews and fieldwork conducted at Church of Scientology sites and especially among schismatic or independent Scientologists who have broken away from the church and in some cases were never members in the first place (Thomas 2021).

Finally, the scholarship and other professional contributions of Massimo Introvigne, an Italian sociologist and managing director of the Center for Studies on New Religions (CESNUR), deserve special mention (e.g., Introvigne 2017c). The annual conferences held by CESNUR have offered NRM researchers a dedicated academic space to explore a variety of topics. Many researchers have presented papers on Scientology at CESNUR over the years, including most of the scholars just mentioned, in addition to some Scientologists, such as the French author and European church spokesperson Eric Roux, who has published academic and popular works (2017, 2018a, 2018b, 2020, 2021). The success of CESNUR and its network has paved the way for other conferences and symposia, such as the First International Conference on the Study of Scientology, sponsored in 2014 by the European Observatory of Religion and Secularism and the Faculty for the Comparative Study of Religion and Secularism in Antwerp, Belgium. The *Journal of CESNUR*, launched in 2017, has already contributed greatly to the study of new religions, including Scientology.

Gaining access to the Church of Scientology is of course easier said than done. Assuming that a researcher obtains permission from an academic IRB, other challenges await. It is not altogether surprising that PR departments within the church might be initially suspicious of would-be researchers in light of the innumerable times that the church has trusted journalists and scholars with sensitive information only to be disparaged in print, television, film, and social media. However, this is not to suggest that journalists and academics find themselves in the same category of outside researchers. On the contrary, compared to academics, journalists find themselves at a decided disadvantage. Hubbard wrote thousands of policies for Scientology organizations in which journalists are described in various unflattering and negative ways. They are "merchants of chaos" or even antisocial personalities known as suppressive persons (SPs) who spread preconceived notions and misinformation (black propaganda) (Hubbard 1972). As Hubbard cautioned:

> In the matter of reporters, etc., it is not worthwhile to give them any time, contrary to popular belief. They are given their story before they leave their editorial rooms and you only strengthen what they have to say by saying anything. They are no public communication line that sways much. Policy is very definite. Ignore. (Hubbard 2007a: 220)

To be clear, this does not mean that Scientologists view *all* journalists as evil or constitutionally incapable of producing a fair and balanced piece. After all, Scientology PR officials occasionally conduct interviews and, more frequently, publish press releases. However, it does explain how Hubbard's stance, now enshrined as scripture and followed by PR staff, has created a built-in obstacle for journalists, filmmakers, and others who seek access to the church. Academics, on the other hand, are not significant features in the Scientology canon, and Hubbard seems to have had relatively positive interactions with academicians during his lifetime, as with the example of J. Stillson Judah. Another instance came in the late 1960s with Hubbard's appreciation of Thomas Szasz, a critic of psychiatry based at the State University of New York (Syracuse), who in 1969 cofounded the church-affiliated Citizens Commission on Human Rights (CCHR) (2021). Academics, it seems, have the potential to fall within Hubbard's more favorable category of "opinion leaders" (OLs) (Hubbard 1971a). From the church's standpoint, sociologists, historians, religious studies scholars, and others are potential PR and legal allies. Other examples include interfaith leaders, politicians, police officers, judges, business executives, and Hollywood celebrities. They are poised to become allies of the church as it seeks to "safe point" (Hubbard 1982a) various sectors of society to allow the unencumbered presence and dissemination of Dianetics and Scientology. This includes ensuring that the church's religious nature is understood and safeguarded around the world, especially in locations where that status may be disputed or lack legal recognition.

The favorable starting position afforded to academicians carries with it a variety of easy opportunities, particularly for researchers who live near a Scientology church. Examples include tours of churches, invitations to local events, and complimentary copies of Hubbard's books and lectures, which, as other scholars can attest, are often sent to teachers and librarians – whether solicited or not. This introductory access is indispensable, but it will likely prove incomplete for those who require a more in-depth understanding of Scientology's teachings and practices and the lived experiences of Scientologists. To gain this kind of access, at least among members of the Church of Scientology, it is imperative to familiarize oneself with the technical vocabulary of the organization so as to converse freely and comfortably with adherents.

One relatively easy way to become familiar with some Dianetics and Scientology jargon is to read through Hubbard's books, especially some of the basics such as *Dianetics: The Modern Science of Mental Health*, *Science of Survival*, *Scientology: The Fundamentals of Thought*, and *Scientology: A New Slant on Life*. The church has also done a good job of explaining specialized terms in works such as *What Is Scientology?* (1999) as well as on its website Scientology.org and videos posted to its Scientology TV channel Hubbard published an extensive *Dianetics and Scientology Technical Dictionary* (1975) and every Dianetics and Scientology text contains an impressive glossary as well as the introductory statement that "In reading this book, be very certain you never go past a word you do not fully understand. The only reason a person gives up a study or becomes confused or unable to learn is because he or she has gone past a word that was not understood" (see, e.g., Hubbard 2007b: "Important Note"). Indeed, according to Hubbard's "Study Technology" (educational philosophy), misunderstood words (MUs) are the most formidable barrier to study, comprehension, and application. I have provided two glossaries – one for terms and another with acronyms – to help the reader with some of the terminology used throughout this work. They are by no means exhaustive but will, I hope, offer a starting point that is useful for the beginning researcher and serve as a springboard for tracking down even fuller glossaries and dictionaries to make the most linguistic sense of the Scientology worldview on its own terms.

I also recommend reading through Hubbard's books and listening to early lectures, ideally in chronological order, for a sense of the growth and evolution of Dianetics and Scientology terminology and practices. This would offer the researcher historical and theological senses of how the mental health therapy of Dianetics transformed into the spiritual world of Scientology and how the two remain interconnected to this day. In the end, though, much like learning a new language – and Hubbard's vernacular arguably does function as both jargon and a kind of dialect – it is perhaps best to immerse one's self, as much as possible, not only into the world of Hubbard's canon but also into Scientology's beliefs as practiced and understood among Scientologists themselves.

It is also necessary to become familiar with the church's internal structures and especially the PR organizations within the Sea Org. This includes the relatively well-known Office of Special Affairs (OSA) as well as a separate group called the Commodore's Messenger Organization (CMO). Sea Org members in the CMO occupy senior management positions in the church and staff the L. Ron Hubbard Personal Public Relations Office (LRH PPRO) (Church of Scientology International 1988).

OSA, in particular, operates as a gatekeeper for academic researchers. Each local church has an OSA representative known as the Director of Special Affairs (DSA), who coordinates PR and legal affairs with the OSA International office headquartered at the Church of Scientology International (CSI) in Los Angeles. OSA officials sometimes attend academic conferences, such as annual meetings of CESNUR and the American Academy of Religion, and have worked with religious studies scholars to produce court statements and publications. One of the more significant examples was the church's *Scientology: Theology and Practice of a Contemporary Religion* (Church of Scientology International 1999), a reference work that also featured articles from theologians, sociologists, and historians. It has since been republished and expanded at websites such as WhatIsScientology.org and ScientologyReligion.org. The relatively congenial relationship between OSA and some in the NRM community has led to the accusation, especially in online anti-Scientology networks, that such scholars are little more than cult apologists or shills for the church. The acrimonious relationship between academics and some Scientology critics is exacerbated by the church's hostility to vocal ex-members (see, e.g., Church of Scientology International 2011).

2 Fieldwork and the Scientological Worldview

My first, albeit passing, encounter with Scientology came in 2000 when I was in high school. While on a field trip to an outdoor mall in Sacramento as part of a visit to the California State Capitol, my friends and I came across a woman who had set up shop along one of the walkways. Copies of Hubbard's *Dianetics: The Modern Science of Mental Health* were neatly stacked and the attendant, as you might guess, turned out to be a Scientology staff member. She was offering free "stress tests" with the use of the E-Meter, the ohmmeter that Hubbard designed based on earlier versions and that is commonly used in Scientology auditing and training. I was skeptical, but one of my friends eagerly took hold of the E-Meter cans as we watched the needle on the meter move back and forth while the staff member adjusted the knobs and claimed to pinpoint areas of stress. The friend, genuinely interested, described areas of distress in her life – family problems, trouble in school, and so on – and was impressed by the staff member and especially the ways that the needle swayed back and forth, sometimes rising, sometimes falling, and moving at different speeds. This apparently indicated some kind of precision and measurement. The whole experience lasted no more than a few minutes. None of us bought *Dianetics*, and I do not even remember the staff member being all that aggressive about making a sale. Maybe she assumed we did not have any money, or maybe she was simply happy that someone stopped to speak with her and learn more firsthand.

Scientology would not appear on my radar again until I began work on my doctorate in religious studies in 2010. At Claremont Graduate University, I took a class with the historian and Mormon studies scholar Richard L. Bushman entitled "American Scripture: From Thomas Jefferson to L. Ron Hubbard." We studied texts and traditions from a number of mainstream and marginalized religious traditions such as Mormonism, Christian Science, and Scientology. At the time I was planning a dissertation related to Mormon history and ecumenical dialogue, but I became increasingly interested in L. Ron Hubbard and Scientology. After taking the class I decided to explore the Church of Scientology's connections to Mormon studies.

One of the early projects that brought me into contact with Scientologists in Los Angeles involved comparing religious advertising among Mormons and Scientologists, especially in light of the similarities between the "I'm a Mormon" and "Meet a Scientologist" campaigns that existed at the time. To learn more about the Scientology side, I sent off an email to the PR department at the CSI. Soon after I received a response that launched my adventure into a world that has taken up much of my time and energy over the past decade. The representative who emailed me back was very pleasant and happy to answer my questions about the "Meet a Scientologist" campaign (Church of Scientology International 2021a), which included short videos of parishioners talking about their lives and successes with Dianetics and Scientology. These videos are still available at the Scientology.org website and on the more recent Scientology TV streaming platforms.

I ended up interviewing a Sea Org member over the phone and also took a lengthy and productive tour of the Church of Scientology of Los Angeles and the American Saint Hill Organization, both located near Sunset Boulevard and Vermont Avenue. I presented a paper on the Mormon and

Scientology campaigns at conferences, including the 2011 Sunstone Symposium at Weber State University, and was interviewed about it by a public radio station in Salt Lake City. Overall, it was a positive experience and the radio program was well received by the Sea Org members with whom I had talked – despite their objection that I had focused too much on individualism in Scientology and not enough on community-wide and humanitarian programs.

After that first successful academic adventure into Scientology, I had an ambitious idea: what if the Church of Scientology would give me permission to interview members and even do some fieldwork? I floated the idea to some Sea Org members and there seemed to be some interest, so I wrote up a proposal, including a list of interview questions, which were IRB approved, and mailed it to the CSI in Los Angeles. I waited and waited – and waited some more. A few months went by and still no response. I had pretty much given up hope and began to think about other possible dissertation topics. I followed up one more time on the proposal to check in and, to my surprise, I was invited to a lunch meeting in Pasadena with one of the Sea Org members as well as the PR director at the Church of Scientology of Pasadena. Most of the visit involved catching up and chitchat, and at the very end I was invited to begin the project by conducting the first interviews at the Pasadena church.

Those interviews ended up being very successful. I soon got into a nice rhythm as an interviewer and became increasingly familiar with Scientology culture, teachings, and lingo along the way. Wishing to capitalize on those successes, I funded my own travel across the country and conducted as many interviews as I could. Most lasted for an hour or more, some up to three and four hours, and I was thrilled that Scientologists were open to speaking with me on the record. I interviewed and took tours everywhere I could – Los Angeles, Clearwater (Florida), New York, Washington, DC, Salt Lake City, Las Vegas, San Jose, Phoenix, Portland (Oregon), Florence (Kentucky), and Bay Head (New Jersey). I even traveled to England to visit the London Fitzroy House and Saint Hill facilities in East Grinstead. In the end, I conducted sixty-nine formal interviews and must have spoken with several hundred more Scientologists, including parishioners, staff members, Sea Org members, even a few ex-members, either informally or off the record in the course of tours and follow-ups in that blitz between 2011 and 2013. That project served as the basis of the book *Among the Scientologists* (2019), which included analysis of the interviews and excerpts from church members on a variety of themes: L. Ron Hubbard, David Miscavige – the church's current leader and head of its Religious Technology Center (RTC) that polices orthodoxy and orthopraxy – Dianetics, Scientology, Sea Org membership, confidential scriptures, money donated, previous religious affiliations, and many other personal and socioeconomic items.

Learning the Tech

I also gained permission to take Scientology courses and proceed up the Bridge to Total Freedom, most of which was completed at the Church of Scientology Celebrity Centre International in Hollywood in 2012 and 2013. For several months during this period, I spent most of my days at CC, as it is known, sometimes for ten or more hours at a time. I had a great time diving in and could not have asked for a better way to learn about and experience Dianetics and Scientology from the inside out. I came to an informal agreement with the PR head at CC not to advertise my status as a PhD researcher among Scientologists and it was also mutually agreed that I was there for personal and not merely academic reasons. Church policy would have otherwise prevented me from receiving auditing and taking classes. I explained to the CC OSA representative that I was indeed interested in the value of Dianetics and Scientology as both a participant and observer and I was allowed to proceed on that basis.

First, I completed the Dianetics (Book One) Seminar, which included learning about the basic principles of Hubbard's original text and especially how it was practiced in 1950 without the use of the E-Meter, a later addition. That seminar included delivering *and* receiving 1950s-style auditing, with the auditor seated across from the "preclear" (the one receiving counseling). Next came the "Book One Co-Audit," where participants are invited to continue co-auditing, as it is called, for as long as they would like with partners in the seminar. I spent several weeks co-auditing Dianetics and occasionally made use of the techniques presented in another early Hubbard work, *Self Analysis* (Hubbard 2007b, originally published 1951). During this period I also completed several introductory classes that required study of Hubbard's written materials in a class setting with course supervisors tasked with ensuring comprehension and application, per church policy (Westbrook 2015: 127–30). Courses included "Success through Communication," "Personal Efficiency," "Formulas for Living," "Ups and Downs in Life," "How to Get Motivated," and "Personal Values and Integrity." I also managed to finish more than a dozen extension courses, all based on Hubbard's books and lectures such as *Dianetics, Science of Survival, Scientology: A History of Man, Advanced Procedure and Axioms*, and *State of Man Congress*. I completed these and many other courses at home, with lessons emailed in to a course supervisor for grading and feedback.

The most intensive activities I completed were the Purification Rundown and Objectives Processing, the first two major steps on the Bridge to Total Freedom (which is taken up at greater length in Section 3). The Purification Rundown, or "Purif," required me to first visit a medical doctor for a checkup to ensure that I was physically prepared. That program took about three weeks to complete with a regimen that consisted of running, taking doses of niacin, vitamins, oil, and lecithin, and then sitting and sweating out toxins in a sauna for five hours a day (cumulatively), with periods in between to cool down or shower as needed. The experience is considered complete when the individual no longer exhibits a niacin flush after a 5,000 mg dosage, an amount that is reached gradually over the course of the program. The goal or "end phenomenon" (EP) of the Purif, according to the Bridge to Total Freedom chart, is "Freedom from the restimulative effects of drug residuals and other toxins" (Church of Scientology International 1998, also online). I underwent the Purif in my late twenties and for the most part found it beneficial and rejuvenating, although there were some days, especially in the beginning, when I went home quite tired – evidence, from a Scientological perspective, that I was indeed "running out" toxins. Maybe I did remove harmful chemicals. At the very least, I enjoyed the time in the sauna and socialized with a variety of Scientologists as we progressed together, some of whom, quite interestingly, had completed the Purif years before and were redoing it as a prerequisite for more advanced auditing on the Operating Thetan (OT) levels.

After the Purif I made my way to the next step on the Bridge, then referred to as "TRs and Objectives" and as of late 2013 included as part of the "Survival Rundown." Training routines/drills (TRs) are the basic exercises used to train auditors, involving communication skills to ensure that auditing proceeds in a smooth fashion without the auditor thrown off or distracted by anything the preclear may say or do. At this level I was introduced to the basic TRs and practiced each one of them with a "twin" (partner) over the course of two weeks, until a course supervisor marked them as complete. It was a long process and for the most part involved sitting across from my partner as we practiced the questions or commands on one another and perfected the techniques. Some of the training involved moving around the room to work on particular commands related to intention and bodily control.

With the TRs under our belts, my twin and I began the central part of the auditing itself – that is, Objectives Processing – with the goal to become "oriented in the present time of the physical universe" (Church of Scientology International 1998: 181). That may sound like a simple or mundane task, but completing Objectives took several months of hard work, with days that alternated between delivering and receiving auditing. I observed that others took even longer – sometimes more than a year based on their availability to co-audit due to work, school, family, and other responsibilities. Depending on the particular process carried out, which was monitored by a course supervisor in the room and then managed by a case supervisor at the end of each day, my twin and I could be found sitting, standing, or walking around the CC campus. Our sessions usually took place indoors, although the procedure occasionally permitted working outside as we put our attention on objects and people as directed. For instance, a particular command might be as simple as "look around here and tell me something you could have," "look around here and tell me what you would permit to remain in place," or "look around and tell me with what you could dispense." These examples collectively are known as CCH 8, which stands for Communication, Control, and Havingness, number 8 (Hubbard 2007c: 152, 1975: 62).

Training routines and Objectives involved an enormous commitment of time and energy and gave me personal insight into the investment that Scientologists put into their mental and spiritual progress. As I have written elsewhere (Westbrook 2019: 33–39), it can take many years, and quite often decades, to advance up the Bridge to Total Freedom to Clear and then to the OT levels. It usually also requires fees (or "fixed donations," as the church calls them) ranging from thousands of dollars at the lower levels to hundreds of thousands for advanced auditing. Objectives processing was lengthened by the need, on a co-auditing basis, to take meticulous notes during each auditing session. These notes were then cleaned up and placed in my partner's preclear (PC) folder for review by an anonymous case supervisor in preparation for auditing in the next session. Another factor that helps account for the time commitment is the need to visit an examiner after each session. The examiner is a staff member who ensures that someone is on track or done with auditing after a session by using the E-Meter to check for a floating needle (F/N) along with "good indicators" (GIs) such as cheerfulness, smiles, and contentment with the session. If these are absent, the preclear would need to return to session in the next twenty-four hours and continue auditing to a point when the individual would meet the examiner's (i.e., Hubbard's) standards for successful auditing. I should add that I paid for my own introductory courses, Purif, and Objectives auditing. This was per Hubbard's policy that services cannot be given away for free, although it is possible for someone else to pay one's donations or to receive auditing in exchange for volunteer service on staff or in the Sea Org. The financial investment in my case came to about $3,000 in 2012/13, and I am told that the fixed donation rates for the Purif and Objectives – the latter of which is now referred to as the Survival Rundown or SRD – have increased in recent years.

After completing Objectives Processing, I was ready for the next step on the Bridge, the Scientology Drug Rundown, the EP of which is to be "released from harmful effects of drugs, medicine, or alcohol" (Church of Scientology International 1998: 181). This step is notable because it is the first to involve the auditor's regular use of the E-Meter. I could not afford a new meter – about $5,000 at the time – but my Objectives partner found a way to borrow one from a Scientologist friend. By this point, however, I decided to conclude my fieldwork and auditing at CC and focus more attention on completing the next steps of my doctoral program. I later completed a course at the Church of Scientology of Pasadena, the "Basic Study Manual," based on Hubbard's study technology, especially the "three barriers to study," namely *lack of mass, too steep a gradient*, and, most insidiously, *misunderstood words* (MUs) (Church of Scientology International 2021b). But for all practical purposes, I wrapped up the interviews and fieldwork in 2013 and turned my attention to writing, graduating, and teaching in religious studies, with special attention to new and alternative religions.

L. Ron Hubbard among the Scientologists

Oral history is labor intensive but worthwhile. My doctoral work focused on the lived religious experiences and personal histories of ordinary – rather than celebrity – Scientologists. But L. Ron Hubbard invariably came up in the interviews, not so much in biographical terms but with an eye to the founder's meaning in their spiritual development. After all, to apprehend Dianetics and Scientology is to some extent to understand oneself in greater measure and understand – or at least appreciate and admire, in the case of adherents – the creator behind them. As one Scientologist told me when asked if he had met Hubbard, "I feel like I know him because I've traveled so far with him through his works." Another said much the same: "I sure feel like I know him. I've listened to thousands of hours of lectures and read lots of books" (Westbrook 2019: 24).

Many interviewees also described Hubbard's systematic and "scientific" approach to matters of the mind and spirit with an engineer's perspective. They emphasized too that he was an extraordinary man – rather than a prophet, messiah, or deity – who, like a preeminent navigator, carefully charted the paths to Clear and OT. As Hugh Urban has observed (2011: 26–56), Hubbard had an uncanny entrepreneurial ability to study other systems of belief – ancient and modern, Eastern and Western – and synthesize features that he found workable into the complex theology and practices of Dianetics and Scientology. As one church member explained to me: "He's not a religious figure like a god or

a messiah or anything like that. He was a man but he was no ordinary guy."
According to another church member, Hubbard should be thought of "as an
engineer ... he basically solved the problem of the mind." Many
Scientologists, in support of Urban's point, acknowledged the ways in which
their founder, as one member put it, "didn't invent any of this. This is all real
phenomena that existed long before he came along." Yet another parishioner was
even more blunt: "Who cares if he stole from other religions? He was trying to
make it so it was more streamlined, so that people could live better."

Scientologists' understanding of Hubbard as an explorer and engineer of the
mind and spirit is certainly in line with how he viewed himself. Long before
Dianetics and Scientology, Hubbard briefly studied engineering at George
Washington University (1931–32) and earned entrance to the prestigious
Explorers Club in New York City (Westbrook 2019: 68, 244n114). Of course
he was also a well-known writer, most famous for his SF. However, he wrote in
a number of genres, including Western, fantasy, adventure, horror, mystery, and
romance. Sometimes forgotten is that his most famous work in the SF field,
Battlefield Earth (1982b), followed by the ten-volume *Mission Earth* (1985–87),
came only in his later years, decades after Scientology organizations had taken
root and spread around the world (Bigliardi 2017). To be sure, there are strong SF
themes to be found in Scientology's theology, most obviously in the space opera
cosmology of the OT levels, but also at lower and more public levels, such as
Hubbard's lectures from the 1950s and 1960s, including "The Role of Earth"
(1997) and "The Free Being" (2009a). After all, Hubbard's most widespread early
presentation of Dianetics came with the article "Evolution of a Science" in the
magazine *Astounding Science Fiction* (1950a; republished 2007d), edited by John
W. Campbell, himself an early Dianetics enthusiast.

Hubbard's popularity as a pulp author and his targeting of *Dianetics* to an SF
audience obscures the fact that he presented earlier versions of Dianetics theory
to niche and academic audiences in the early years (see, e.g., Hubbard 2007e,
2012b, 2012c: 19). One notable example was the article "*Terra Incognita*: The
Mind," a much shorter piece than the one in *Astounding Science Fiction*, which
appeared in the winter–spring issue of *The Explorers Journal* (1950b). Hubbard
crafted the article with Explorers Club colleagues and friends in mind, and it
surely had a more limited audience compared to the many thousands Campbell
reached in *Astounding Science Fiction*. Nevertheless, it is revealing on
a number of levels, particularly because it advances the author's vision of
himself as an explorer and adventurer. Hubbard begins the article by positioning
exploration in internal rather than merely external terms. "Probably the stran-
gest place an explorer can go is inside," he wrote. "The earth's frontiers are
being rapidly gobbled up by the fleet flight of planes, the stars are not yet

reached. But there still exists a dark unknown which, if a strange horizon for an adventurer, is nevertheless capable of producing some adventures scarcely rivaled by Livingston" (Hubbard 1950b: 1).

In an age when explorers would soon turn their attention to outer space, Hubbard saw himself as a pioneer on a different scale, uncovering truths about an unknown or unexplored territory, or *terra incognita*, "that vast and hitherto unknown realm half an inch back of our foreheads," as he soon after put it in *Dianetics: The Modern Science of Mental Health* (1950; republished 2007f). What he uncovered, discovered, recovered, or invented, depending on how you look at it, became nothing less than the raw ingredients of a worldview that were combined, repackaged, and offered up according to the rules of a new mental health movement and, eventually, a new religion for the world. Susan Raine has written about Hubbard's colonialism and "quest for empire," including "strategies for controlling both the immaterial and material dimensions of humanity" (Raine 2017: 1), observations that might be said of other religions and religious founders as well, especially those with missionary and global ambitions. Another source on Hubbard's outlook as an explorer – indeed even as a heroic and quasi-savior figure – came in a 1966 interview he gave to fellow Scientologist Tony Hitchman well after Scientology churches had replaced Dianetics.

> I've slept with bandits in Mongolia and I've hunted with pygmies in the Philippines, as a matter of fact, I've studied 21 different primitive races, including the white race, and my conclusions were that man, regardless of his state of culture and so forth, was essentially the same, that he was a spiritual being that was pulled down to the material – the fleshly interests – to an interplay in life that was in fact too great for him to confront. And I concluded finally that he needed a hand. (Golden Era Productions 2006)

In 1966 Hubbard also penned "My Only Defense for Having Lived," which provided additional autobiographical details and served as another chance to emphasize that Dianetics, Scientology, and movement up the Bridge to Total Freedom ultimately concern self-knowledge: "My intentions in life did not include making a story of myself. I only wanted to know Man and understand him. I did not really care if he did not understand me so long as he understood himself" (Hubbard 2012b: 140).

3 Pilgrimage and the Bridge to Total Freedom

Although the notion of pilgrimage is not explicitly taken up by Scientology's founder, L. Ron Hubbard, his step-by-step Bridge to Total Freedom is intended to provide church members with a distinct spiritual path leading to the states of

Clear and OT. In order to walk this spiritual path, individual Scientologists must physically journey to a series of Scientology churches where auditing, a form of spiritual counseling, and auditor training levels are delivered in a graded fashion. In addition, the church has established what it refers to as "L. Ron Hubbard Landmark Sites" for members and interested outsiders to tour key historic sites in the development of Dianetics and Scientology. These sites have no direct soteriological value but are educationally, culturally, and spiritually significant – to both Scientologists and researchers – because they allow visitors to "walk in Ron's footsteps" (Church of Scientology International 2014) and retrace the evolution of Hubbard's research, writing, and practices.

Scientologists eschew language such as *belief* or *faith* in describing the role of Hubbard's teachings and practices in their lives, preferring such terms as *knowledge, technology,* and *workability* (Westbrook 2015, 2019). This insistence speaks to the original scientific methodology that Hubbard claimed for Dianetics and the scientific sensibilities that carried over into the spiritual realities one encounters via auditing on the E-Meter. After all, he described Dianetics and Scientology as *technologies.* Linguistic distinctions between mere belief (personal, subjective, privatized) and knowledge (objective, verifiable, public) are hardly novel and have been a feature of religious traditions and self-legitimation since the Enlightenment. This distinguishes the Scientologist's gnostic appeal to self-knowledge from other traditions that have appealed to the legitimating power of science in their names (e.g., Christian Science, Religious Science, and the Moorish Science Temple of America) more than their methods and practices. Indeed, in one source Hubbard defined Scientology as "the study and handling of the spirit in relationship to itself, universes, and other life" (Hubbard 2007c: 5).

Kocku von Stuckrad refers to this modern phenomenon and legitimating sensibility as the "scientification of religion" (Stuckrad 2014: 178–82), but in the case of Scientology the phrase *sacralization of science* may also be accurate. Indeed there seems to be an ongoing and dialectical relationship between science and religion in Hubbard's writings, lectures, and praxis, which I suspect is one reason why it has been difficult for laypersons and scholars to directly apprehend Scientology's religious and philosophical characteristics (see, e.g., Bainbridge 1987; Dericquebourg 2010; Lewis 2010, 2015). Arguably one of Hubbard's contributions with Scientology was to break down the barrier between scientific (objective, external) and religious (subjective, internal) forms of knowledge, offering instead what has been called an "applied religious philosophy" and "spiritual technology" within the church (Westbrook 2019: 17–18). At the same time, and paradoxically, Dianetics and Scientology are designed to provide personal spiritual progress gauged by a radically subjective epistemology: "Nothing in Scientology is true for you unless you have observed it and it is true according to your observation" (Hubbard 1961). Scientology's sense of technology is neither replicable nor falsifiable in the modern senses of those terms, as early studies of Dianetics demonstrated (Winter 1951; Fischer 1953; Fox, Davis & Lebovits 1959). However, for Scientologists, this misses the point that the ultimate purpose of Hubbard's "Tech" is mental and spiritual awakening and growth, not peer-reviewed validation.

To an outsider it may seem as though Hubbard was increasingly deified after his death in 1986, with busts of the man present throughout Scientology organizations and an Office of LRH located in every church. However, the Scientologists I encounter make clear that Hubbard is the founder of Dianetics and Scientology and the systematizer of eons of spiritual wisdom, but no more divine than all Scientologists can become by fully walking the Bridge to Total Freedom to OT that he designed, codified, and refined during his lifetime. This amounts to a hierarchy in which LRH is both the "Source" of Dianetics and Scientology as well as the model OT, inviting others to follow his path in ways comparable to other spiritual guides and gurus. In fact, because of some writings hinting in this direction, Hubbard is popularly considered among Scientologists as a Buddhistic figure and possibly even a future Buddha (Maitreya) (Hubbard 1974).

Hubbard repeatedly invited Scientologists to spiritually progress from preclear to Clear to OT, often couched in the language of friendship and assistance. As he put it in his 1982 statement "From Clear to Eternity," "for you, my dearest friend, I've done what I could to make it good for you" (Hubbard 2007g: 433). To be an OT is to approach a state of godliness in which one is "at cause" over the confines of matter, energy, space, and time (MEST). As one OT VIII explained during an interview, moving up the Bridge is a "trip up the Tone Scale and across the dynamics" (Westbrook 2019: 119). Scientologists understand the eighth dynamic as the urge to survive in the context of "Infinity," divinity, or the "God Dynamic." The specific nature of this dynamic is theoretically left up to the member himself or herself. Hubbard's own scriptures, however, especially his lectures, describe one's native state as a thetan in godlike terms. In fact, according to his cosmogony, the universe itself exists because of the continual co-creation of omnipotent thetans who work in agreement and creative unison (Hubbard 2009b, 2010). To become an OT, then, is to rediscover this true nature and to recover unlimited spiritual potential, despite the encumbrances of the physical universe that thetans unwittingly created in the first place.

The highest OT level currently available, OT VIII, is considered the first real OT level, with the preceding seven counted as pre-OT levels. The next two levels, OT IX and OT X, are scheduled to be released once all Scientology churches have reached the "size of Old Saint Hill," referring to the East Grinstead organization during the 1960s. Thus the journey to OT is still in development in church practice. Moreover, advancement up the OT levels has taken on both sociological and theological significance. For instance, the Flag Land Base in Clearwater, Florida, encourages movement up the Bridge in part because it will contribute to the goal of putting ten thousand solo auditors on and through OT VII. Scientologists view this as a tipping point after which the "theta/entheta ratios" of the planet will shift in favor of theta and drastically speed the progress of "planetary Clearing" (Church of Scientology Flag Service Organization 2010, 2021). This urgency clearly serves as an incentive for pilgrimage and migration to Florida because it advances an individual as well as a humanitarian purpose.

The L. Ron Hubbard Landmark Sites

While the L. Ron Hubbard Landmark Sites have only been open to the public since 2005, they are gaining traction as pilgrimage sites for the purpose of educating Scientology members about the development of Dianetics and Scientology. In line with Scientologists' purpose to remain true to "Source" (i.e., Hubbard and the technologies he codified in his nonfiction writings counted as scripture), the sites have been impeccably restored by the church to reflect the conditions when Hubbard lived or worked in them, and accordingly they have received numerous awards from historical and preservation societies. Just as Scientologists dedicate their lives to following Hubbard's instructions on Dianetics and Scientology – most prominently as mandated in his "Keeping Scientology Working" (1965) – so also have church-directed preservationists paid attention to the minute details of restoration for the edification of visitors. More than sites of pilgrimage, the landmarks are also intended to facilitate historical and theological appreciation and perhaps even encourage Scientologists to return home with a renewed sense of purpose for themselves and others. In the words of the preservationist and naturalist Freeman Tilden, "The chief aim of interpretation is not instruction, but provocation" (Tilden 2008: 15).

This task is accomplished by using sources such as photographs, architectural schematics, and oral histories gained from members who knew and worked with Hubbard and, in the case of the Bay Head, New Jersey house, chemical analysis replicated even the color of paint on the walls. The church has released videos outlining some of these preservation efforts, and these serve as introductions to the historical significance of the sites themselves (Church of Scientology International 2021c). All of the sites are managed and curated by members of the Sea Org, who typically reside at the locations as well. While cared for by Scientologists, the sites are owned by Heritage Properties International, an entity associated with the Church of Spiritual Technology (CST), the organization responsible for archiving and preserving Hubbard's legacy for use by future generations. This relationship attests to the importance of the sites to Scientologists, as CST and its affiliated staff members are highly respected within the church for their privileged role in the fields of archiving, preservation, and restoration.

In order of chronology in the story of Dianetics and Scientology, the present heritage sites are located in Bay Head, New Jersey (1950); Phoenix, Arizona (1952–55); Washington, DC (1955–59); London, England (1956–59); East Grinstead, England (1959–67); and Johannesburg, South Africa (1960–61). Other sites will likely be restored and added as time goes on. There are many candidates for possible inclusion, including real estate that could be purchased or restored from Hubbard's adult years in Havana, Cuba (1951); Wichita, Kansas (1951–52); Philadelphia (1952–53); New York City (1930s, 1960s); Florida (1975); and California (1970s–1980s); not to mention possible locations from his youthful years, including Tilden, Nebraska (1911); Helena, Montana (1913); Washington, DC (1923–24); and Bremerton and Seattle, Washington (1925–27). In fact, any geographical space connected to Hubbard's biography is theoretically open to acquisition as a landmark site. Along these lines, in recent years the Church of Scientology Religious Trust – which is fundraising for an L. Ron Hubbard Hall to be constructed in downtown Clearwater, Florida – has sponsored trips for Scientologists to visit some of the lesser-known sites in Hubbard's life and church history. These include George Washington University (Washington, DC), Puerto Rico, New York City, Boston, Philadelphia, Seville (Spain), and the Canary Islands (Church of Scientology Religious Trust 2021). The most recently opened churches, called Ideal Organizations, contain modern information centers with video displays detailing Hubbard's life. In addition to celebrating particular chapters in Scientology's history, the current landmark sites display artifacts and videos on the founder's life as a whole. Perhaps the primary museum dedicated to celebrating and disseminating information about Hubbard's life and influence is the L. Ron Hubbard Life Exhibition, open daily for tours and located on the ground floor of the CSI building in Los Angeles.

In the discussion that follows I trace the steps of what can be considered a pilgrimage into the origins and evolution of Dianetics and Scientology via the

LRH Landmark Sites as they currently exist. This survey of the historic sites amounts to a brief introduction to the intellectual history of Hubbard, the Church of Scientology, and the Bridge to Total Freedom – extending from Bay Head, New Jersey (1950), to Johannesburg, South Africa (1960). Of course an account of this decade is by no means an exhaustive account of Scientology history and readers are referred to other histories to fill in gaps in the biographical and institutional narratives (see, e.g., Melton 2009; Urban 2011: 39–46, 60–77, 82–88, 162–77; Westbrook 2019: 67–75, 77–85, 96–102, 127–40, 166–72). Still, the history of these sites offers the researcher a window into periods of Hubbard's life as well as the church's presentation of itself and of its founder's legacy.

In late 1949 Hubbard rented the summer home of James C. Kellogg III in Bay Head, New Jersey, for the purpose of researching and writing a volume on the human mind that would become *Dianetics: The Modern Science of Mental Health*. Located on the Jersey Shore, the house has three stories and "eight bedrooms here to wander around and contemplate," as Hubbard wrote to his friend and fellow writer Russell Hays in November 1949 (Hubbard 2012c: 22). On May 9, 1950 – now considered a holiday and celebrated annually within the church – Hubbard published *Dianetics*. The book set forth the goal of a Clear, someone free of psychosomatic illnesses and in particular free of moments of pain or unconsciousness (engrams) that are the source of aberrant behavior and collectively comprise the irrational "reactive mind" (whose opposite is the rational or "analytical mind") (Hubbard 2007f).

The goal of Dianetics as a therapeutic method is to remove these engrams and thus rid the individual of the stimulus–response nature of the reactive mind that every individual has as a holdover from earlier periods of human evolution, when it was advantageous in fight-or-flight situations. The 1950 work was itself the culmination of Hubbard's philosophical and clinical research on the human mind, and it served as a handbook for the grassroots training of auditors, with Dianetics centers soon opening in Los Angeles, Phoenix, Washington, DC, Honolulu, and Wichita. The book shot to the top of the *New York Times* bestseller list in 1950 and remained there for more than twenty-six weeks.

Hubbard wrote the five-hundred-page *Dianetics* in the Bay Head house in less than one month on his Remington typewriter. The typewriter is on display in one of the bedrooms at the site, a testimony to Hubbard's capacity as a prolific writer who typed more than a hundred words per minute. The rest of the site provides the Scientology visitor with many other opportunities to walk in Ron's footsteps, including the dining room where Hubbard met with the likes of John W. Campbell, editor of *Astounding Science Fiction* – an early and staunch supporter of the Dianetics movement – and others, such as the author

Theodore Sturgeon and the mathematician Claude Shannon. Hubbard even supervised early Dianetics students, including Campbell, in some of the bedrooms in the house.

The second floor of the house has been converted into a private display with conversation rooms where chapters of Hubbard's life are presented along with information about the church's social betterment and humanitarian programs, including The Way to Happiness (based on Hubbard 2007j), Applied Scholastics, Narconon, Criminon, and so on. The second floor also contains, as do all of the landmark sites, an impressive library of texts that Hubbard referenced during the historical and developmental period in question. In the Bay Head house, for instance, one finds books by Will Durant, Sigmund Freud, Alfred Koryzsbki, William Shakespeare, Jean-Martin Charcot, Francis Bacon, John Dewey, Edward Gibbon, Immanuel Kant, Herbert Spencer, and Voltaire, among others, signifying to the visitor the founder's familiarity with classical intellectuals and theorists. This in turn legitimizes and even sanctifies the space, providing historical context to Hubbard's unique accomplishment in the field of mental health.

The landmark site in Phoenix, known as the Camelback House, is located less than two miles from the Church of Scientology of Phoenix. While Bay Head is considered the birthplace of Dianetics, Phoenix is the birthplace of Scientology because it was there in the early 1950s that Hubbard moved beyond his research into the mind, conducted in New Jersey and Wichita, and into his research into an individual's spiritual nature. Dianetics remained the antecedent of Scientology and became a central feature of the Bridge to Total Freedom, as discussed later in this section. But in Phoenix, Hubbard rebranded his research under this new name for legal as well as theological reasons (Westbrook 2019: 83–85). He delivered dozens of lectures in the area and also pioneered the use of machinery in quantifying and handling sources of mental and spiritual travail – what became the E-Meter, based on a prototype by the Dianetics student and inventor Volney Mathison. The "Phoenix Lectures" given during this period have particular significance for Scientologists, in part because Hubbard outlined an intellectual and religious history that traced its roots to Asian traditions such as Buddhism, Confucianism, and Taoism (Hubbard 2007h). It was also during this time that he lectured and experimented more widely to produce out-of-body experiences for his preclears – what he termed exteriorization or the process of "going exterior" – that is, exterior to the body, which is a vessel for the soul or thetan (Hubbard 1975: 151, 2007i).

Scientologists visiting the house today find it restored to its mid-1950s state, complete with identical furniture and furnishings, and even a fully operational vintage car sitting in the driveway. In the living room the visitor gains a distinct sense of LRH's presence during the period by a number of unique features, including a restored piano he used to play for guests and, most striking to me, an early version of the E-Meter with "soup cans" attached. For Scientologists familiar with the most recent meter – Mark VIII Ultra, released in late 2013 – this is a tangible reminder of the machine's history and evolution. In fact, during his time in Phoenix, Hubbard experimented with other forms of technology that did not survive or become normative features of auditing and auditor training.

One also finds a Geiger counter in the house, which Hubbard used to measure radiation levels due to the proximity to nuclear testing sites in Nevada. As Hugh Urban has discussed, Dianetics and Scientology were born in a postwar and, in particular, a Cold War climate, within (and against) which Hubbard operated (Urban 2011: 89–117). His concern with the threat of nuclear war resonated with the fears of Americans at large, and visitors to Camelback are now aware of the extensive nuclear testing that occurred at the Nevada Test Site (Nevada National Security Site) well into the 2000s (Johnson 1984). In 1957 Hubbard coauthored a book on the subject of radiation (*All About Radiation*), and in the late 1970s and early 1980s he developed the sauna-based Purif as a means to rid the body of toxins, including those caused by sources of radiation, whether from the sun, microwaves, or nuclear radiation. In 1958 the Food and Drug Administration (FDA) raided a church affiliated distribution center in Silver Spring, Maryland, and confiscated twenty-one thousand tablets of "Dianazene," since it was claimed that they afforded protection from radiation poisoning (Westbrook 2019: 97). Troubles with the FDA continued, leading, for instance, to a 1973 ruling that there must be disclaimer on the E-Meter indicating that the device "is not medically or scientifically useful for the diagnosis, treatment or prevention of any disease" (Westbrook 2019: 97–100). The Purif, meanwhile, became a fundamental step on the Bridge to Total Freedom. While developing a nascent Scientology theology, Hubbard was also keenly aware of the socio-political milieu in which the United States operated, evidently becoming interested in preserving and extending the life of the body. This concern is expressed in the title of another, later text, *Clear Body, Clear Mind* (1990).

By 1955 Hubbard had relocated Scientology operations to Washington, DC, which is chronologically home to the next landmark, the (Original) Founding Church of Scientology. The site is located near the church's National Affairs Office, opened in 2012, and the former site of the local church, which is within walking distance of the church currently used by local Scientologists – all located in the DuPont Circle and Embassy Row areas.

There were at least two reasons for the relocation to Washington, DC. On one hand, the move aligns with Hubbard's desire to expand Scientology and the Washington, DC, area provided the chance to be near political authorities, personalities, and centers of communication that might legitimize the new religion and its stated goal of spiritual egalitarianism. In fact, this church was founded on July 4, 1955, as a testament to Hubbard's cognizance of the historical significance of the new home and his apparent intention to weave the history and purposes of Scientology into the grander narrative of American values. On the other hand, Hubbard is also clear that the relocation was undertaken to remove Scientologists and the church management from excessive radiation. "The central headquarters of this organization," he said in a lecture in Washington, DC, in 1957, "were moved from Arizona only because grand pianos began to count like uranium mines … Everything was alive and radioactive. Dust blew you in the face at night and you'd have a sunburn, but there was no sun. Now, that's just too much radiation" (Hubbard 2009c). While he was certainly successful in providing a safe space for a headquarters, the church in Washington, DC, faced threats from the US government, most prominently in the form of conflict with Vice President Richard Nixon, who sent Secret Service agents to harass the Washington, DC, church following the unauthorized inclusion of Nixon's name in a Scientology periodical (Westbrook 2019: 101). By the 1970s the Church of Scientology's antagonism toward the government had reached such a fearful state that members with a notorious (now defunct) department within the church, the Guardian's Office (GO), broke into federal offices in Washington, DC, and stole documents related to Hubbard and the church. The FBI responded in July 1977 by raiding churches in Washington, DC, and Los Angeles. A number of Scientologists were later imprisoned for their involvement, most notably Hubbard's wife, Mary Sue, who was a senior GO leader (Urban 2011: 109–12, 167–70; Westbrook 2019: 159–64; STAND League 2021).

The historic site in Washington, DC, probably receives more non-Scientology visitors than any of the other landmark sites, given its location in the nation's capital and the existence of dozens of museums in the area that attract tourists from around the world. Scientologists who visit the original founding church – the FCDC, Founding Church of Scientology, Washington, DC – find the site to be a window into Hubbard's unique contributions to Scientology during his years in the District of Columbia. As a young man, he briefly attended college at George Washington University, during which time he attended a course on atomic and molecular phenomena and later remarked that this sent him on a journey thinking more about the nature of *élan vital*. This connection is made to the visitor with display cases on the first floor.

Also on the first floor, and more germane to Scientology proper, is a small room that Hubbard used to deliver some of the lectures known internally as the "Advanced Clinical Course Lectures" (ACCs), where more advanced auditing students were taught the latest techniques in a more intimate setting. These lectures, as with all Hubbard's works on Dianetics and Scientology, are considered church scripture, so touring this room provides yet another opportunity to observe the setting of the birth and development of a new religion. This room was also the chapel where Hubbard performed marriages and naming ceremonies, with pictorial evidence on display alongside the Scientology cross with eight points representing the Eight Dynamics. The space also contains two Ampex tape recording machines used to record hundreds of reel-to-reel lectures delivered during this period.

The upper floors principally contain the original Hubbard Communications Office, complete with a mimeograph machine and a distribution center, from which books, pamphlets, lectures, and other church materials were sent internationally. The tour of these areas provides a glimpse into the momentum of Scientology in the mid-to-late 1950s and the assembly-line sense in which Hubbard's latest policies or bulletins on a particular topic were rolled off and disseminated in rapid sequence. The founder's personal office is nearby, complete with mostly original items placed exactly according to photographs taken by Hubbard's secretary during the time in question. The office is both decidedly cosmopolitan and "exotically" international – a large globe positioned nearby, a diverse personal library, ancient Tibetan Buddhist texts on the bookshelf, and other items across the room, such as an eight-hundred-year-old Mongolian war drum from Genghis Khan's army, African-themed statues, and a Zulu spear and shield. During this time, and until 1966, Hubbard held the title of Executive Director, and one gains the sense that the space was, in effect, the epicenter of the Scientology universe. The hundreds of "Hubbard Communications Office Policy Letters" and "Hubbard Communications Office Bulletins" bearing the name Washington, DC, remind visiting Scientologists of the site's importance for the growing church.

In 1956 the Hubbard Association of Scientologists International (HASI) purchased Fitzroy House in the Fitzrovia neighborhood of London to serve as the new international headquarters of Scientology organizations. In some of his lectures Hubbard remarked that the city was chosen because it was a communications center with a desired and needed global reach. "You can get to all parts of Scientology from England faster than from the United States," he told an audience in December 1961 (Hubbard 2009d). He seems to have run Scientology operations from Washington, DC, up to March 6, 1959, which at that time was home to the FCDC. By March 10, however, there is a clear switch and letters are written from Fitzroy, signaling that Hubbard himself had permanently moved to the area, again underscoring the obvious centrality – and indeed the necessity – of his authoritative presence in church administration.

Scientologists visiting Fitzroy House are given a tour in which the house is put into historical context and are told about the great number of literary luminaries who once lived in the neighborhood: H. G. Wells, George Orwell, Charles Dickens, Virginia Woolf, and George Bernard Shaw (the last of whom lived in the same building). This serves to position Hubbard as a similarly eminent writer, given his own prolific body of fiction and nonfiction works. Indeed, Guinness World Records (2022) lists him as the record holder for most published works by a single author (1,084 publications).

The five-story building served as the first "Hubbard Communications Office Worldwide" (HCO WW). The reception area on the first floor contains displays about Hubbard's life and especially his activities in London. One of the most memorable items is an original sign that reads "Letters or messages posted here to go to L. Ron Hubbard immediately," which, during Hubbard's life, was known internally as "Standing Order Number 1" – namely, that all mail sent to the founder would be received and responded to by his personal office (Westbrook 2019: 265n54). The presence of this sign serves to emphasize Hubbard's everyman accessibility and the fact that he considered himself a friend to humanity in its quest for mental and spiritual freedom.

The house contains other artifacts and areas, such as wax-based recording machines, restored secretarial offices, former course and auditing rooms, and a preserved LRH office. As with the Camelback House, the office houses an early version of the E-Meter, a British green and gold model that is smaller than the one in use today. This older model is notable because it was used to establish case histories of past lives, which Hubbard compiled in *Have You Lived Before This Life?* (Hubbard 1989, originally published in 1958). For Scientologists, recalling experiences of past lives – known as whole track memory – is one of the most spiritually important ways of demonstrating the workability of "the Tech," as members put it. However, in the end, as insightful as Fitzroy is to the broader story of Scientology, members recognize Hubbard's forward propulsion that led to the creation of the next site as his new home.

By June 1959 we find one of the first Hubbard policy letters mentioning East Grinstead, Sussex, UK, and soon after he described Scientology's administrative relocation and provided updated contact information to international Scientology mission holders (Hubbard 1959a). The next month, he had provided little information about the relocation beyond what was required clerically and administratively. "We have just moved a small staff of HCO WW down to Saint Hill," he simply reported, "and this is the place from which your bulletins will be coming and out of which we will be operating" (Hubbard 1959b).

More information came on September 14, 1959, in the form of a New Bulletin, in which Hubbard detailed the importance of the still fledgling operation in East Grinstead. "Here, on half a hundred acres of lovely grounds in a mansion where we have not yet found all the bedrooms, we are handling the problems of administration and service for the world of Scientology," the bulletin relayed. "We are not very many here and as the sun never sets on Scientology we are very busy thetans." The bulletin goes on to say that there were only nineteen staff members at that time and solicits others to join, noting that "Saint Hill needs all manner of assistance." Because of the serene English locale, an outsider would not suspect that the manor was home to "some of the most dedicated people on Earth" (Hubbard 1959c).

Today, Scientologists visiting Saint Hill Manor, or Saint Hill, as it is generally known, recognize Hubbard's statement as prophetic given the size and present-day importance of the East Grinstead complex in the international consciousness of church members. Technically, Saint Hill Manor is but one building – albeit an important one – on the property owned by the church that is today formally and internally known as the Advanced Organization Saint Hill United Kingdom (AOSH UK). The AOSH UK is staffed by Sea Org members, and it is the only place in the United Kingdom where Scientologists can journey from the first steps of the Bridge to Total Freedom to OT V, after which they need to travel to Clearwater, then the *Freewinds* vessel. The property also annually hosts the event that celebrates the anniversary of the founding of the International Association of Scientologists in October 1984.

Its early claim to fame was that it became the next center of the Scientology universe by virtue of Hubbard's guiding presence, which attracted the large number of students who gravitated to the manor in the early to mid-1960s. At Saint Hill, he developed numerous pieces of what I have elsewhere argued ought to be viewed as an incipient systematic theology (Westbrook 2015) while acknowledging that Hubbard did not call it such and that he referred to his work in more scientific terms (Lewis 2015: 235–38). Key documents and concepts such as "Keeping Scientology Working" (orthodoxy), the original version of the Bridge to Total Freedom (soteriology), SPs and disconnection (theology of evil), overts and withholds (theology of sin), barriers to study (misunderstood words, too steep a gradient, and lack of mass, as part of his educational philosophy), and writings about the TRs (used in auditor training) trace most substantively and foundationally to the Saint Hill period. These and other subjects were taken up in the course of what Hubbard called the Saint Hill Special Briefing Course (SHSBC), which is still offered in East Grinstead, Los Angeles, Copenhagen, Sydney, and Johannesburg based on audio recordings.

The chapel where the original SHSBC was delivered is available for tours; weddings and naming ceremonies are conducted there as well.

Saint Hill Manor is perhaps best and most simply known to Scientologists as Hubbard's home (see Figure 1), since he also lived on site and maintained other interests, such as driving a prized 1960 XK 150-S Jaguar (restored and on display in the garage), pursuing professional photography (his restored darkroom is part of the tour), and playing the organ and piano (housed in his restored office). Arguably even more than Fitzroy House, the manor has an illustrious history of its own, including the immediate past owner, the maharajah of Jaipur. The visitor is struck by the building's ornate architecture and interior, including the walls of the ballroom painted in the late 1940s by John Spencer Churchill, nephew of Winston Churchill. It is nicknamed the Monkey Room due to the depiction of one hundred and forty monkeys at play against an Arcadian backdrop.

At the end of 1960, having established Saint Hill as Scientology's new world headquarters, Hubbard made a trip to Johannesburg, where he stayed until the following year. The transition seems mostly justified by the fact that he had an English-speaking, predominately White, audience, which incidentally was the same advantage he held when visiting and lecturing to Scientologists in Australia (see, e.g., Doherty & Richardson 2019: 66). However, another reason is that England was becoming increasingly inhospitable due to pressures on the government to investigate the church. Hubbard therefore viewed South Africa as a possible place for the church to more safely reestablish central operations. His home during this period, the Linksfield Ridge House in Johannesburg, is also a landmark site. While it is certainly the farthest from the major population centers of Scientologists found in places such as Los Angeles, Clearwater, East Grinstead, and Copenhagen, South Africa has a sizable population of

Figure 1 L. Ron Hubbard, Saint Hill Manor, East Grinstead, 1964. Photograph by John Fudge. Rights held by Edward E. Marsh. Courtesy of Edward E. Marsh.

Scientologists and in 2019 opened a new Advanced Organization and Saint Hill for the country and the continent (Church of Scientology International 2019).

Sojourners to Linksfield Ridge House will see that the house, much like the ones in Bay Head and Phoenix, is situated in a residential neighborhood. There Scientologists learn of Hubbard's radical plans in 1960 and 1961 to end apartheid in South Africa by authoring a "one man, one vote" constitution for the country, though, not surprisingly, it failed to gain traction with politicians (Rothstein 2017: 115; Westbrook 2019: 251n38). South Africa did not live up to Hubbard's high hopes at the time to become the next major center of Scientology, and in 1966 he spent time in Rhodesia (present-day Zimbabwe), likewise seeking without success a new and sustainable base of operations. By 1967, searching for another solution, he assembled a group of dedicated Scientologists who formed the Sea Project (later the Sea Org) and took to the Atlantic and Mediterranean to continue his research into the spirit, one well-known expression of which was the discovery of the OT III materials. During this entire period, however, Hubbard continued to develop aspects of systematic theology in key ways. By 1975 the Sea Org had relocated to Florida and he remained in the United States for the rest of his life (Westbrook 2019: 137–40, 166–68).

The Bridge to Total Freedom as Pilgrimage Guide

In 1965, while at Saint Hill, Hubbard released the first version of what would later become the Bridge to Total Freedom. In a relatively rare videotaped lecture, he released the "Classification Gradation and Awareness Chart of Levels and Certificates." It was a unique systematic achievement for Scientologists who until this point had lacked a single, stable source to follow Hubbard's path for mental and spiritual self-realization. This first chart and subsequent revisions are methodologically based on the premise, punctuated in his Study Technology, that education and understanding take place in sequential fashion.

"Life is improved on a gradient," he told the audience in East Grinstead. "It's improved a little and then it's improved a little more and it's improved a little more and a little more . . . You want a gradual grade up. That's what gradation means in our particular sense" (Hubbard 2008). In other words, the steps on the Bridge must be followed precisely in the order Hubbard codified or else one will falter and fail to make the proper and maximized spiritual progress. This hermeneutic naturally resonates with Gnostic, esoteric, and Buddhist soteriologies, with which Hubbard seems to have had at least some familiarity based on his studies and experiences (Kent 1996; Flinn 2009; Grünschloß 2009).

At the same time, Hubbard's path to enlightenment provides a democratized route that is both modern and ancient in orientation. It is modern in the sense that it exhibits Hubbard's methodical and technological approach to mental and spiritual problems. It is a precise recipe for spiritual gain – a one-size-fits-all model. In point of fact, Dianetics and Scientology are trademarked and copyrighted, and in 1982 one of the church's lawyers contended to American church leaders that Hubbard's creations are analogous to the Coca-Cola brand and that his spiritual writings and techniques similarly contain trade secrets (Church of Scientology International 1982; Westbrook 2019: 32).

The content and shape of the Bridge have remained much the same despite multiple versions since 1965. There are two sides – *training* and *processing*. These roughly correspond to the training of auditors and the receiving of auditing itself. As Scientologists made clear to me, this is because Hubbard envisioned all Scientologists as auditors, or spiritual counselors, so the two sides of the Bridge made it possible to train and then become competent to deliver auditing to others, in particular through *co-auditing*.

On a practical and lived level, Scientologists begin walking on the Bridge for a variety of reasons and in an abundance of ways. This becomes apparent from a study of the chart itself, which is found in every Scientology organization with a copy also available online (Church of Scientology International 1998). The latest version was published in 2013, based on restoration efforts known as the Golden Age of Technology Phase II. There are introductory routes, which are typically short courses or seminars based on topics such as Dianetics, communication, Study Technology, parenting skills, personal integrity, and financial well-being. Most, but not all, are relatively secular in orientation before one moves to the first major step on the Bridge, the Purif, from which one proceeds to receiving some form of training to use the E-Meter as it is required on the lower half of the Bridge. It is a necessity when one reaches the OT levels that require solo auditing, where the individual is *both* the auditor and pre-OT, meaning he or she holds the meter cans in one hand and monitors and records the session in the other.

Given the fact that Hubbard personally developed and authorized auditing methods based on his own experiences as an auditor and preclear/pre-OT, the Bridge provides a very concrete sense that one is walking in Ron's footsteps. One also develops a growing sense of gratitude and allegiance to the Tech as one advances and experiences spiritual gains. These advances belong squarely and uniquely to the Scientologist but they are based, as a matter of method if not content, on Hubbard's own mental and spiritual path to enlightenment. This may imply that the journey up the Bridge, which is supposed to be a journey of increasing spiritual freedom, is in fact one of increasing allegiance, even subservience, to Hubbard's particularized sense of the self and one's place in the cosmos. However, for the Scientologists I have encountered in the United States, the exact opposite is true. Namely, they are thankful to LRH for discovering and systematizing a path to enlightenment that they feel awakens them to their true selves – unhampered by "past baggage," as one member described it.

The geographical path by which members advance up the Bridge is to a large extent based on the availability of churches, missions, and field auditors. In addition, there are Scientology Volunteer Ministers, who are found throughout the world delivering basic auditing (such as Touch Assists) at sites of disaster and acute need. However, it is primarily through the matrix of field auditors, missions, and varying types of churches that Scientologists progress up the Bridge in the proper and full sense. It is common, for instance, for missions to be located in urban areas, and CSI claims thousands of locations around the globe, providing a website to search for locations (Church of Scientology International 2021d). Often a stress test table is located on the street near the mission, or a sign is placed outside the mission advertising a free personality test. After participating in these activities, the interested person may take an introductory course. Scientology Missions International (SMI) provides administrative guidance to the network of missions, which, like all other organizations connected to Scientology, are separately incorporated but accountable to SMI (Rigal-Cellard 2009).

Field auditors occupy a position that is technically below that of the missions and their staff. They exist to cover greater geographical ranges – for instance, rural areas where there may be few Scientology resources. Typically they audit out of their homes or travel and make house calls. The International Hubbard Ecclesiastical League of Pastors (I HELP) provides institutional guidance to the network of thousands of auditors operating in the field. The services offered in the field depend on the training of the particular auditor, and much the same limitation is imposed on mission locations, which, for instance, could offer New Era Dianetics (NED) services on the way to the state of Clear, assuming that there is a properly trained staff member at the levels of Class V or Class VI auditor. In other words, dependent on location and availability, one could receive auditing in the field and at missions to advance through the following steps on the Bridge to Total Freedom: Purif, Survival Rundown, Scientology Drug Rundown, Happiness Rundown, ARC Straightwire, Grades 0 to IV, New Era Dianetics, and Expanded Dianetics.

In practice, however, Scientologists typically receive the majority of these services at the next level of churches, the Class V Organization, which are fewer in number and exist primarily in major metropolitan areas. While one can receive Dianetics auditing at lower ecclesiastical levels, Class V churches and above offer the Clear Certainty Rundown (CCRD), a prerequisite for Bridge advancement. Scientologists often commute to these churches or move closer for convenient access. The Ideal Organizations that have opened since the 2000s are Class V churches in cities such as New York, Los Angeles, Clearwater, Nashville, Madrid, London, Berlin, Rome, Brussels, Johannesburg, Mexico City, Melbourne, Tel Aviv, Sydney, Basel, and Kaohsiung, Taiwan, among many others. In these locations Scientologists can advance to Clear and undergo training to become auditors themselves, up to Class V.

The OT levels above Clear are offered at Advanced Organizations (AOs), which are delivered in far fewer locations and, as a result, necessitate long-distance travel for many Scientologists. At present, AOs are located in Los Angeles, Clearwater, East Grinstead, Copenhagen, Sydney, and Johannesburg, with auditors available to translate services into dozens of languages to accommodate international travelers. Travel to AOs is done on short- and long-term bases, depending on how far the individual seeks to progress at a particular time. As mentioned, part of the preparation for the OT levels is training on the E-Meter in order to solo audit. (For those who do not reach Clear through Dianetics auditing on the Bridge, Hubbard designed a separate "Clearing Course" for the purpose of solo auditing to Clear, also offered at AOs.) The primary services offered are solo auditor training, OT levels I–V, and Class VIII auditor training, the highest level achievable by Scientologists outside the Sea Org. With the exception of the solo training, these levels contain confidential data and such materials are not allowed out of the course room, where they are kept behind locked doors requiring key card access. Advancement to any of the OT levels is contingent on an invitation from the RTC, offered on the basis of the pre-OT's spiritual and ethical readiness.

Once OT V, a Scientologist next ventures to the Flag Land Base (Flag Service Organization) in Clearwater, since it is the only location that offers the training and delivery of OT VI and OT VII. However, OT VII is unique in that it is solo audited either at Flag or, more typically, in one's own home. This is convenient because OT VII is also one of the longest steps on the Bridge, and for this reason it is colloquially referred to as "The Level." Solo auditors "on 7" go in session a few times daily, usually for twenty to thirty minutes at a time, and send auditing worksheets by mail to Clearwater for review by a case supervisor, who provides ongoing instruction and guidance. Sending in material by mail (instead of email) is required by Flag for security purposes. Indeed, since the materials are confidential, solo auditors lock away written materials when not in use and even have house alarms to prevent unauthorized access. However, OT VII is not entirely home-based. Twice a year, the solo auditor returns to Flag for a "refresher" – confessional auditing, known as Security Checking, combined with classroom instruction – which typically takes one or two weeks to complete. As a result of this biannual commitment, which can last for years depending on one's progress, it is common for members to relocate to Clearwater.

In 2013, the church opened its new Flag Building in Clearwater, an impressive cathedral of 377,000 square feet that occupies a city block and now delivers the bulk of services, including some recently released "Flag-only rundowns," namely the Cause Resurgence Rundown and Super Power Rundowns. In total, the Flag Land Base consists of about fifty buildings and two million square feet, positioning it as a major and ever-expanding center for Scientologists. Increasing numbers of international Scientologists in the area attest to this appeal, and auditing from the bottom of the Bridge to OT VII is delivered in more than two dozen languages to meet the need and attract sojourners. For instance, of the approximately twenty-three hundred Sea Org staff at Flag, sixteen hundred are non-Americans, and non-Sea Org international communities exist in the form of nationally based "OT Committees." Some of the most significant migratory sources are Russia, Italy, Hungary, Mexico, Canada, and Taiwan. Though the phrase seems to have lost use in recent years, the Flag Land Base has been referred to by Scientologists as the "Mecca of Technical Perfection" or "Pinnacle of Technical Perfection" in recognition of its status as a spiritual gathering place where Hubbard ensured that Scientology would be most "standardly" delivered (1971b).

Finally, the most senior ecclesiastical Scientology entity, at least with respect to the delivery of auditing, is the motor vessel *Freewinds*, which houses the Flag Ship Service Organization (FSSO). Commissioned in 1988, the 440-foot ship is based in the Caribbean and delivers all available services, up to and including OT VIII, which again is considered the first of the actual OT levels – the preceding technically are pre-OT. Notably, most Scientologists visiting the *Freewinds* come for services other than OT VIII, in part because it is a distraction-free environment that allows for complete immersion into spiritual self-development. The choice of a cruise ship for the delivery of the first OT level is all the more appropriate given that Hubbard researched some of the preceding OT levels aboard the *Apollo*, at sea in the Mediterranean (1967–75). For this reason the church refers to it as an oasis "off the crossroads of the world" (Ward 2014; Church of Scientology International 2021e). Not surprisingly, some of the most popular courses offered on the ship are those based on Hubbard's lectures about the nature and potentialities of the OT. Unencumbered, an OT is "at cause" over (or in control of) the component parts of the physical universe – MEST.

Even at OT VIII, the path up the Bridge is by no means complete. The current chart lists OT IX through XV. As noted, once all Class V Organizations reach an organizational state termed "Saint Hill Size" – that is, the high productivity of auditing and training found at the original Saint Hill organization in the 1960s – OT IX and X may be released and presumably delivered on *Freewinds*. Until then, OT VIIIs and others high on the Bridge are viewed as opinion leaders in the church who can return home with a reinvigorated sense of purpose to expand the church in their locales (Hubbard 1971a). This will in turn speed up the cause of Planetary Clearing so that others may also make the journey to OT and beyond. In the end, then, OT VIIIs have, for all practical and immediate purposes, realized Hubbard's goal to become like him. At this point they are poised to similarly function as teaching guides, as embodiments of the pilgrimage up the Bridge. Returning home around the world, they can bear witness to the efficacy of Hubbard's technologies, encouraging preclears and pre-OTs in their communities to likewise walk in Ron's spiritual footsteps.

4 Archival Research

This section presents a guide to resources on Scientology that are available in public and private archives. Some of these archival materials are easy to access, given the wealth of sources available at American public universities such as University of California, Los Angeles, University of California, Santa Barbara, Ohio State University, and San Diego State University, among others. However, challenges exist, such as the lack of digitized materials and restrictions in place at some university collections.

Surely the most difficult archives to visit are the private ones managed by the church – for example, in Los Angeles, Gilman Hot Springs (California), and Clearwater – since these are not presently open to the public or to academic researchers. I suspect it is unlikely that the church will trust an outside researcher with access to its archives, at least for the foreseeable future. This is due in large part to information control as well as the confidential and sensitive materials involved (such as any OT data, which is only made available to initiates on the upper levels of the Bridge to Total Freedom and within a secure setting).

However, it may someday be possible for a Scientology researcher to gain access or collaborate with church officials and other relevant parties, such as the officially designated LRH biographer, a lay Scientologist named Dan Sherman. Another possibility is that scholars will have to wait until a new generation of OSA and CMO PR leadership emerges within the church. They will be drawn from the church's second-, third-, and even fourth-generation membership, both in and out of the Sea Org, some of whom may be open to more substantial biographical projects, historical analysis, and interdisciplinary religious studies perspectives.

The good news for Scientology studies researchers is that an abundance of materials is available in libraries and archives, much of which has still not been analyzed or written about in the secondary literature (see, e.g., Christensen 2009; Frenschkowski 2010). This includes Hubbard's extensive fiction and especially his nonfiction writings, such as books and policy letters, not to mention the thousands of Hubbard audio recordings (e.g., the Basics lectures, Congress lectures, and ACC lectures). Fortunately, PR officials, particularly those in OSA, are often quite willing to donate most of these materials to academics, and they are often accessible in many public and academic libraries. There are also more specialized materials in university archives. In the rest of this section I want to survey some of these holdings. In Appendix B I have consolidated some of the most relevant English-language collections, with links to the latest finding aids where available.

San Diego State University

The San Diego State University (SDSU) Special Collections and University Archives is home to numerous collections relevant to the academic study of Scientology and alternative religions at large. The SDSU holdings in SF are particularly strong, especially the materials found in the Edward E. Marsh Golden Age of Science Fiction Reading Room found on the ground floor of Love Library. The Marsh Room is worth the trip alone, and researchers will find that Hubbard plays a major, though by no means exclusive, role alongside other SF giants such as Frank Herbert, Ray Bradbury, Forest J. Ackerman, Isaac Asimov, Arthur C. Clarke, Robert Heinlein, L. Sprague de Camp, E. E. "Doc" Smith, and A. E. van Vogt. However, this room houses only a fraction of the Scientology holdings that have been donated over the years, especially from Scientologist, philanthropist, and SDSU alumnus Edward E. Marsh. Notable Scientology-related finds at SDSU include rare and first-edition Hubbard fiction and nonfiction (many of which are signed), E-Meters from different eras, runs of magazines such as *Aberee, Celebrity, Freewinds, Advance,* and *International Scientology News,* and complete sets of books and lectures, including the entire Saint Hill Special Briefing Course (SHSBC). One can also find several banker boxes full of correspondence from *Astounding Science Fiction* editor John W. Campbell, some of which is relevant to understanding Hubbard and especially the early Dianetics years. SDSU's longtime head of special collections, Robert Ray, now retired, built up this collection for many years and ensured that the university will remain an important research center for Scientology studies, Western esotericism, and perennial wisdom (San Diego State University 2022). I suspect that it will only continue to grow in scope and stature in the years to come.

University of California, Santa Barbara

In terms of breadth and depth, the holdings related to Scientology and other new religions at the University of California, Santa Barbara's (UCSB) Special Research Collections are quite possibly without rival. Of special note is the immensely valuable and diverse American Religions Collection assembled over the decades by J. Gordon Melton, whose Institute for the Study of American Religion was headquartered in Santa Barbara before Melton took up a position at Baylor University and relocated operations to Texas. As with the SDSU collections, UCSB has benefited from librarians and archivists who particularly value American religious diversity. This includes David Gartrell, an archivist and subject liaison for religion studies, who is tremendously helpful and knowledgeable. The American Religions Collection – an astonishing 270 cartons according to the Online Archive of California – contains no shortage of Scientology books, lectures, periodicals, and ephemera that are well worth exploring. One of the more unusual finds I came across during a visit to UCSB were copies of a journal published by the California Association of Dianetic Auditors (CADA) and edited by A. E. van Vogt, who did not follow Hubbard as he transitioned to the religion of Scientology and instead worked to promote Dianetics and advance it as a scientifically valid therapeutic technique. In addition, UCSB is notable for holding the files of the now defunct Cult Awareness Network (CAN), which was bankrupted and dissolved in 1996 due to a number of legal battles with the Church of Scientology. The CAN collection effectively offers a historical snapshot of the "cult wars" of the 1970s through 1990s. Scientology researchers will be particularly interested in the large numbers of letters received by Scientology parishioners who sought membership in the CAN. The organization denied access, however, which led to legal action on the basis of discrimination.

University of California, Los Angeles

The University of California, Los Angeles (UCLA) Special Collections is another important center, which is not altogether surprising given that the greater Los Angeles area is home to the largest concentration of Scientologists in the world, second only to the Tampa Bay area in Florida. Unlike at SDSU and UCSB, material related to Scientology is mostly, if not entirely, housed off site, so the visitor will need to request materials in advance based on reading findings aids, searching online, or communicating with archivists and staff. Two of the most relevant collections are devoted to the Church of Scientology and focus on the 1950s to 1980s and the Louis Jolyon "Jolly" West Papers, donated by the longtime psychiatrist, professor, and critic of Scientology. Other holdings also may be of interest, such as tape recordings in the Aldous and Laura Huxley Papers. One of the most useful sources I encountered, though one that I was not allowed to copy, was an oral history interview conducted with A. E. van Vogt by Elizabeth I. Dixon (van Vogt 1964), since it offers tremendous insight into the history of Dianetics in California.

Graduate Theological Union, Berkeley

Further north, the Graduate Theological Union (GTU) in Berkeley houses a strong set of collections that are less well known but worthy of scholarly attention. The GTU played an important role in the early academic study of NRMs. One important presence was J. Stillson Judah, a librarian at the GTU and a scholar of alternative religious groups such as ISKCON. In fact, I initially made the trip to the Bay Area because I wanted to listen to the audio file of an interview that Judah conducted with Hubbard in Washington, DC, in 1958. It is housed in the GTU Library's Special Collections. This interview is a very early example of a religious studies researcher doing work on Hubbard and Scientology. A transcript is available from the Church of Scientology, most recently published in *Philosopher & Founder: Rediscovery of the Human Soul* (Hubbard 2012a: 87–91). Searching through finding aids, and with assistance from a GTU archivist, I came across an even rarer find, an apparently full run of the "Orders of the Day" (OODs) that Hubbard and Sea Org staff released during the *Apollo* years at sea in the Mediterranean, Portugal, and elsewhere in the late 1960s and early 1970s before making their way to the Caribbean and finally Florida by 1975. These offer valuable insights into daily life in the Sea Org as well as Hubbard's leadership style during this period, before he retreated even further from public view once back in the United States.

Other Collections

These are by no means the only collections with Scientology materials, and researchers are advised to consult ArchiveGrid, WorldCat, governmental databases, and others for more information and any recent acquisitions. Two additional sets of resources are the Hugh B. Urban Scientology Collection at Ohio State University and the Westbrook Scientology Collection at the Claremont Colleges Library. There are also collections outside the United

States. Edward E. Marsh, who donated materials to the SDSU Special Collections, also maintains an impressive private library, in Mexico as of 2022, centered around Hubbard and other figures from the Golden Age of SF. Another archive that deserves mention is the massive collection on alternative beliefs and religions housed at the University of Alberta Library in Canada, where Stephen A. Kent makes material available on a restricted basis to undergraduate and graduate students. It is also possible that archival materials, inside and outside the United States, may be digitized and shared on demand – depending on copyright, donor, and privacy considerations – helping remove barriers to access in the digital age.

5 Target Two

After a mixed and at times tumultuous history, the Church of Scientology seems increasingly open to dialogue and cooperation with researchers. This emerging state of the field may not be obvious to newcomers, given the inordinate attention Scientology receives in the media from critical and antagonistic sources, but others more familiar with the study of new religions can attest to a gradual shift over the past few decades (see, e.g., Urban 2010; Westbrook 2017a) that has brought us to this stage of "Scientology studies 2.0" (Introvigne 2020) some three and a half decades after Hubbard's passing. Hubbard once wrote to his followers that he would move on to an undisclosed (and extraterrestrial) "Target Two" in the next lifetime, where he would have the opportunity to continue his work (Hubbard 1982c). In a similar vein, many opportunities are available in Scientology studies as the subfield continues to gain momentum among researchers, both inside and outside of the study of new religions, as Scientologists carry forward Hubbard's legacy well into the twenty-first century.

To be sure, obstacles remain, especially as the church attempts to promote a particular image of itself in society and meanwhile retains, at least among many academics, a lingering reputation for interference in research and writing (Graham 2014). As Douglas E. Cowan helpfully urged, "*Respond* to the product, certainly, disagree with it, debate it, excoriate it, if that's what Scientologists want to do – that kind of exchange lies at the heart of the scholarly dialectic. But do *not* interfere with its production" (Cowan 2009: 73). More than a decade after Cowan's remarks, first presented at an international CESNUR conference in 2004 (Cowan 2009: 73), the Church of Scientology seems to have passed through at least some of its growing pains and has been in its current post-Hubbard phase, under the leadership of David Miscavige since the late 1980s, for even longer than Hubbard guided the church during his own lifetime. The increase in scholarship over the past decade, much of it produced independently of the church's cooperation, input, or knowledge, may encourage even more historical, theological, and sociological research on this American-born religion moving forward (Doherty 2020; Roux 2020).

Despite these obstacles, there are numerous productive paths forward for Scientology studies students and scholars in the twenty-first century, including many that require little or no direct access to the church or Scientologists. One of the more obvious topics for study is the life and legacy of L. Ron Hubbard, who has still received relatively little biographical attention among professional historians, religious studies scholars, SF researchers, and others (see, e.g., Christensen 2005; Melton 2009; Rothstein 2014; Introvigne 2018b, 2019; Nevala-Lee 2018; Camacho 2020; Kent 2020). Researchers interested in the church's presentation of Hubbard's life are advised to visit the LRH Life Exhibition on the ground floor of the CSI building in Los Angeles and read through the sixteen-volume L. Ron Hubbard Series published by Bridge Publications in 2012. Hubbard's birthday, March 13, is an official holiday in the church, and it is also a date when the church's LRH biographer, Dan Sherman, speaks at an international event about the founder's legacy (Westbrook 2019: 25). In addition to Hubbard's "My Only Defense for Having Lived" (Hubbard 2012b) and the L. Ron Hubbard Landmark Sites discussed in Section 3, other biographically relevant sources include "My Philosophy" (Hubbard 2012d), an interview on Granada Television (Hubbard 1968), and publications from the church-affiliated (though apparently defunct) "Old Timers Network" (2000).

Another large and multifaceted area for research is the church's social engagement and humanitarian outreach. Some of these efforts have received academic attention, such as by Rigal-Cellard (2019: 72–107) and Westbrook (2017c), but much more work remains on these programs. They include the Citizens Commission for Human Rights (CCHR), Applied Scholastics, Volunteer Ministers, The Way to Happiness, Criminon, Narconon, Truth about Drugs, and Youth for Human Rights International, among others (Church of Scientology International 2021f). Further research should also be carried out on secularized expressions of Hubbard's work, such as the World Institute of Scientology Enterprises (WISE), which supports the use of his managerial and administrative techniques in the workplace. Although the Church of Scientology does not sponsor a four-year educational institution, it does support the Hubbard College of Administration International, which is headquartered in Los Angeles and offers certificate programs and an associate degree. Hubbard's philosophy of "management by statistics" is found in other systems, but his version, including the use of the "organizing board" (org board), sheds light on productivity in both business and religious contexts (Hubbard College of Administration International 2020; Church of Scientology International 2021g).

Looking beyond the church, independent Scientology remains another open and fascinating area that has been explored more in recent years (e.g., Thomas 2021). From the church's perspective, attempts to practice a reformed or independent version of Scientology are not only impractical and misguided but fundamentally evil, since they subvert the purity of Hubbard's technologies exactly as he developed them. For independent Scientologists, however, it is church members who are the true heretics or "squirrels," to use Hubbard's term (Hubbard 1958). These outside groups go by names such as independent or Indy Scientology, the Free Zone, or Ron's Org, the last of which refers to a network, mostly in Europe, that dates back to the early 1980s. In the history of Dianetics and Scientology there have been dozens of splinter groups, most of which have gone extinct or morphed into other forms – from Synergistics, Idenics, the Process Church, and *est* (Erhard Seminars Training) to Kenja Communications, the Advanced Ability Center (AAC), the Avatar Course, and traumatic incident reduction (TIR) therapy, among many others (see, e.g., Cusack 2017). Some groups were evidently inspired by aspects of Scientology, with one example being Paul Twitchell's synthesis of sources in the creation of Eckankar.

These offshoots and derivations are fascinating in their own right and point to the influence of Scientology as a system on the spiritual and cultural landscape apart from expressions within the contemporary Church of Scientology (see, e.g., Wolfe 2017, 2021; Parenti 2021). It has even been argued that features of Scientology are "quintessentially" American (Kaplan 2006: 96–98), especially when Dianetics and the early church are understood against the historical backdrop of the Cold War (Urban 2011: 89–117). At the same time, Scientology has become a global religion (Rigal-Cellard 2019) and more scholars are paying attention to its history outside the United States, including the United Kingdom, France, Italy, and Australia (see, e.g., Doherty 2013, 2017; Rigal-Cellard 2020).

Numerous other avenues for scholarly exploration exist. Examining the diverse influences on Hubbard in the construction of Dianetics and Scientology might include study of General Semantics, popular psychology, Western esotericism, Theosophy, New Thought, Buddhism, Hinduism, and science fiction, among others (Flinn 2009; Dericquebourg 2017b; Frenschkowski 2017). In addition, there is a need for more research into the particulars of Scientological theology and practices, the experiences of second-, third-, and even fourth-generation members of the church as it moves forward into the twenty-first century, and the ongoing relationship between the Church of Scientology and the Nation of Islam (Muhammad 2013, 2017). Certainly the life and influence of David Miscavige and RTC merit study (Miscavige 2001; Church of Scientology International 2021h). Miscavige, a second-generation Scientologist, is arguably a testament to Scientology's staying power despite no shortage of controversy and negative media attention during his tenure (see, e.g., Westbrook 2018). Church members view Miscavige as the dedicated and rightful "Scientology ecclesiastical leader" in his role as chairman of the board (COB) of RTC. As COB, it is Miscavige's job to maintain Hubbard's intentions as the founder directed (Church of Scientology International 2022). Other possible research topics include lay efforts to communicate about Scientology online (such as Scientology Parent 2021) as well as issues of gender and sexuality among parishioners and Sea Org members. The ethics of studying the confidential OT levels are worth further consideration, including Hubbard's implicit and explicit discussion of them in sources such as the audio recording *Ron's Journal 67* (Hubbard 2005) and the unpublished screenplay "Revolt in the Stars" (Possamai & Possamai-Inesedy 2012). There is also quantitative work to be done on the number of active Scientologists worldwide, acknowledging controversy over methods but recognizing possible standards for measurement such as membership tallies from the International Association of Scientologists and the number of Clears and OTs (Introvigne 2017d; Rigal-Cellard, 2019: 45–53). Continued analysis of "lived religion" among Scientologists (Gregg 2020) is worthwhile, including accounts that incorporate testimonies from disaffected and former members (Rathbun 2013; Shugart 2018; and see Cusack 2020). Of special concern to Scientologists are legal cases regarding persecution and religious freedom violations occurring outside the United States, especially in Germany, France, Belgium, and Russia. The church's efforts to promote its expansion and offerings on television and social media via the Scientology TV channel that launched in 2018 are readily accessible to any researcher with Internet access (Church of Scientology International 2021i). Finally, there is room for more research into the church's response to the COVID-19 pandemic (see, e.g., Šorytė 2020).

The prospects for Scientology researchers have expanded over the past seventy years because of pioneers in NRM studies such as J. Stillson Judah, Roy Wallis, Harriet Whitehead, J. Gordon Melton, James R. Lewis, Massimo Introvigne, Hugh B. Urban, and others. As the subfield of Scientology studies continues to develop, a new generation of scholars – and I suspect even some Scientologists themselves – may be eager to work on some of these open areas and chart new scholarly paths of their own.

Glossary of Terms

Advanced Organization (AO): class of Scientology church where confidential Operating Thetan (OT) levels are delivered. AOs can be found in Los Angeles, Clearwater, East Grinstead, Copenhagen, Sydney, and Johannesburg.

Auditing: the application of Dianetics and Scientology by a trained auditor, to be carried out precisely according to Hubbard's policies and codifications.

Bridge to Total Freedom: also known as the Classification, Gradation, and Awareness Chart of Levels and Certificates or simply the Bridge, it is the step-by-step path designed by Hubbard for the dual purposes of *auditing* and *auditor training*. There are many levels and goals, in particular Clear and Operating Thetan (OT).

Church of Scientology International (CSI): the ecclesiastical "Mother Church" of the Scientology religion, founded in 1981 and headquartered in Los Angeles, California.

Citizens Commission for Human Rights (CCHR): nonprofit organization founded in 1969 by the Church of Scientology to highlight psychiatric abuses and advocate for reform.

Clear (Dianetics): the name of a state achieved in Dianetics auditing, and a term referring to an individual who has achieved this goal per the Bridge to Total Freedom. An individual who is Clear no longer has an irrational "reactive mind" and is in control of the rational or "analytical mind."

COB: Chairman of the Board of the Religious Technology Center (RTC), a position held since 1987 by David Miscavige. In this capacity Miscavige serves as the de facto leader of the Scientology religion.

Commodore's Messenger Organization (CMO): elite unit within the Sea Organization whose members occupy senior management positions. CMO members also staff the L. Ron Hubbard Personal Public Relations Office (LRH PPRO).

Dianetics: mental health theory and therapy developed by L. Ron Hubbard and most famously published in *Dianetics: The Modern Science of Mental Health* (1950). Dianetics is intended to treat psychosomatic illness and has the goal of producing a "Clear." The word *Dianetics* comes from the Greek *dia* (through) and *nous* (mind or soul).

Director of Special Affairs (DSA): Scientology staff member who runs the Department of Special Affairs at a local church. This individual is responsible for local public relations and legal affairs.

Dynamics: eight thrusts toward survival that comprise the totality of an individual's experience in relation to self and the universe. They are: (1) the individual, (2) family/sex, (3) group(s), (4) humanity, (5) life forms, (6) the physical universe, (7) spirit, and (8) infinity, divinity, or God.

E-Meter (electropsychometer): electronic device often (but not always) used in auditing as a means to guide sessions and pinpoint mental and spiritual areas that need to be addressed – and that might not be evident to the preclear's own waking consciousness.

Exteriorization: the act of the thetan (soul) intentionally or unintentionally leaving the body and during which period the individual has varying degrees of perception and other abilities. When this occurs – for instance, in the course of auditing – it is called "going exterior" or "being exterior."

Flag Land Base (FLB): Scientology base located in Clearwater, Florida. It is made up of the Flag Service Organization (FSO), which provides auditing and auditor training services to Scientologists, and the Flag Crew Organization (FCO), which provides support to staff and visitors as well as building services to the organizations in the area.

Floating Needle (F/N): back-and-forth rhythmic movement of the needle on the E-Meter; an indication among Scientologists of the mental and spiritual benefits of auditing, whether during or at the end of a session or auditing level.

Founding Church of Scientology, District of Columbia (FCDC): designation used to refer to the founding Church of Scientology in Washington, DC. It is not the earliest Scientology organization (which dates to 1953 and 1954), but Hubbard gave it this designation since DC was a national headquarters at the time (1955).

Ideal Organization (Ideal Org): another name for a Scientology church but one that conforms to specific staffing, architectural, geographical, and floor plan criteria as outlined by the Church of Scientology International. The phrase comes from an executive directive by Hubbard with the same name.

L. Ron Hubbard Personal Public Relations Office (LRH PPRO): Sea Organization members who promote Hubbard's life and legacy, especially outside the church. They are drawn from the Commodore's Messenger Organization (CMO), an elite unit within the Sea Org.

Office of Special Affairs (OSA): division of the Church of Scientology that interfaces with the broader society, including in the areas of public relations, community outreach, interfaith dialogue, legal affairs, and networking with Directors of Special Affairs (DSAs) at local churches. The Office of Special Affairs International, located in Los Angeles, also works with the church's social betterment and humanitarian programs.

Operating Thetan (OT): ultimate goal of Scientology auditing as listed on the Bridge to Total Freedom. There are currently eight OT levels available in the Church of Scientology. They are confidential and a Scientologist is invited to complete them, in sequence, once Clear.

Preclear (PC): a person being audited who has not achieved the state of Clear and is progressing through levels on the lower half of the Bridge to Total Freedom.

Pre-OT: a person being audited who is Clear or above but not on the actual OT levels. Technically, the pre-OT levels refer to OT I–VII. The first official OT level, OT VIII, was released in 1988. The remaining OT levels (IX–XV) have not yet been released by the Church of Scientology.

Purification Rundown (Purif): program consisting of time in the sauna, a nutrition and vitamin regimen, and exercise designed to purify the body of harmful toxins that might otherwise prevent mental and spiritual progress at later points on the Bridge.

Religious Technology Center (RTC): Scientology organization founded in 1982 and entrusted by Hubbard with the trademarks and service marks of the Scientology religion. It is headed by David Miscavige, who since 1987 has held the position of chairman of the board (COB). Operating from this capacity, he is also the ecclesiastical leader of the Scientology religion.

Scientology: applied religious philosophy created by L. Ron Hubbard. It was predated by Dianetics and developed in the early 1950s. Both Dianetics and Scientology techniques are used in the Church of Scientology today. The word *Scientology* was created from a combination of the Latin *scio* (knowing) and the Greek logos (*study of*), or "knowing how to know.

Scientology Missions International (SMI): "Mother Church" for Scientology mission locations. It is headquartered in Los Angeles and offers direction to the network of missions (small churches) around the world.

Sea Organization: religious order and senior management body of the Church of Scientology, founded by Hubbard in 1967, and whose name owes to its early history aboard ships sailing the Atlantic, Mediterranean, and Caribbean. In 1975 the Sea Organization (Sea Org or SO) relocated to land in New York and in particular Florida, where the Flag Land Base was eventually established in Clearwater. Sea Org members dedicate their lives to church service, even symbolically pledging themselves for a billion years. They serve in churches throughout the world and usually in organizations (churches) staffed by other Sea Org members.

Study Technology: Hubbard's educational methods and philosophy. A key component is recognition of the "three barriers to study," namely (1) *lack of mass*, (2) *too steep a gradient*, and (3) *misunderstood words*.

Suppressive Person (SP): someone who displays a set of antisocial personality traits that have a negative effect on those around them. Hubbard estimated that 2.5 percent of society is composed of SPs who, as a result, have a negative effect on about 20 percent of the population (who as a result are PTS, or potential trouble sources).

Target Two: phrase originally used by Hubbard with respect to plans to export Dianetics and Scientology to another planet in a future lifetime.

Theta: based on the Greek letter theta (θ) and referring in Scientology to thought, life energy, spiritual energy, and the essence of life itself. Its opposite is *entheta*, or enturbulated theta. One of the goals of auditing, in particular on the OT levels, is to increase the amount of theta and thereby positively affect the ratio of theta to entheta in the world.

Thetan: the true nature of an individual as a spiritual being, existing apart from a body, which lives lifetime after lifetime. The ultimate goal of Scientology is to rehabilitate the thetan's inherent and unlimited abilities so that it can operate fully and without encumbrance.

Tone Scale: scale of emotions with numerical values assigned to each, used in Dianetics and Scientology as a systematic means to predict human behavior and determine the effectiveness of different types of auditing on a given individual. It is described in Hubbard's early Dianetics writings and most systematically in *Science of Survival* (1951).

Training Routines (TRs): exercises developed by Hubbard to train auditors and improve communication skills.

Twin: partner in Dianetics and Scientology auditing and training.

Whole Track: Hubbard's phrase for recollections and occurrences from past lifetimes. It is a more expansive term than "time track," which appeared in early Dianetics writings. A number of whole track (past life) incidents are described in Hubbard's *Scientology: A History of Man* (2007k; first published in 1952 as *What to Audit*) and can include the thetan's (soul's) experiences from billions, trillions, and even quadrillions of years ago, both on Earth and across the universe.

Glossary of Acronyms

AO:	Advanced Organization
CCHR:	Citizens Commission on Human Rights
CMO:	Commodore's Messenger Organization
COB:	Chairman of the Board (i.e., David Miscavige)
CSI:	Church of Scientology International
CST:	Church of Spiritual Technology
DSA:	Director of Special Affairs
FCDC:	Founding Church, District of Columbia
FLB:	Flag Land Base
F/N:	floating needle
LRH:	L. Ron Hubbard
LRH PPRO:	L. Ron Hubbard Personal Public Relations Office
MEST:	matter, energy, space, and time
OSA:	Office of Special Affairs
OT:	Operating Thetan
SMI:	Scientology Missions International
SP:	suppressive person
RTC:	Religious Technology Center
TRs:	training routines

Appendix A
Timeline of Major Events in Hubbard's Life and Scientology History/Research

March 13, 1911: Lafayette Ronald (L. Ron) Hubbard born in Tilden, Nebraska. As a child, he traveled extensively with his family due to his father's naval career.

1923: Hubbard introduced to Freudian psychology by Joseph "Snake" Thompson.

1930–32: Hubbard studies at George Washington University in Washington, DC.

1933: Hubbard and Margaret Louise "Polly" Grubb married. They will have two children: L. Ron Hubbard Jr. (later Ronald DeWolf) and Katherine May Hubbard.

February 1934: Hubbard publishes short story in pulp magazine *Thrilling Adventure* and, before the Second World War, publishes more than one hundred other short stories under numerous pen names.

July 1937: First full-length book, *Buckskin Brigades*, published. Other early works include *Fear, Final Blackout,* and *Typewriter in the Sky,* all released in 1940.

1938: *Excalibur* manuscript written, in which Hubbard isolated survival as the lowest common denominator of existence.

Early 1945: After serving as an officer in the US Navy during the Second World War, Hubbard recovers at Oak Knoll Hospital in Oakland, California.

February–March 1946: "Babalon Working" episode with Jack Parsons (OTO) in Pasadena, California.

August 1946: Hubbard and Sara Northrup Hollister married, though the legality is disputed because of an existing marriage with Grubb. Hubbard and Hollister will have one daughter, Alexis Valerie, though this is disputed in Hubbard's last will and testament.

1948–49: *Dianetics: The Original Thesis* distributed as manuscript.

May 1950: "Dianetics: Evolution of a Science" published in *Astounding Science Fiction*, edited by John W. Campbell, an early Dianetics enthusiast.

May 9, 1950: *Dianetics: The Modern Science of Mental Health* published by Hermitage House. It is written in Bay Head, New Jersey – "the birthplace of Dianetics."

June 7, 1950: Hubbard Dianetics Research Foundation established in Elizabeth, New Jersey.

August 1950: Sonya Bianchi presented as the first Clear to an audience at the Shrine Auditorium in Los Angeles.

June 1951–May 1952: Hubbard lectures and publishes in Wichita, Kansas, with financial backing from Don Purcell, who took temporary copyright control of *Dianetics* due to the bankruptcy of the original Hubbard Dianetics Foundation.

1951: *A Doctor's Report on Dianetics* published by medical doctor and early Dianetics enthusiast Joseph A. (J. A.) Winter.

March 1952: Hubbard and Mary Sue Whipp married. They will have four children: Diana, Quentin, Suzette, and Arthur.

May 1952: Dianetics center moves to Phoenix, where Hubbard announces the religious philosophy of Scientology and forms the Hubbard Association of Scientologists International. Phoenix is the "birthplace of Scientology."

1952: Re-evaluation Counseling (RC) founded by Harvey Jackins.

December 1952–January 1953: Philadelphia Doctorate Course (PDC) lectures delivered, primarily in Philadelphia.

April 1953: "The Factors" published by Hubbard.

December 1953: Three churches incorporated in Camden, New Jersey: the Church of American Science, the Church of Scientology, and the Church of Spiritual Engineering.

February 1954: Church of Scientology of California (CSC) founded in Los Angeles, California. (The Church of Scientology International (CSI) traces itself to this founding.)

1954: Hubbard lectures and is based in Phoenix.

July 1955: Founding Church of Scientology founded in Washington, DC, where Hubbard relocates to lecture and write.

1956: Church in Washington, DC, granted tax-exempt status by the United States Internal Revenue Service (IRS).

1958: Hubbard interviewed by academic J. Stillson Judah.

1958: United States Food and Drug Administration (FDA) seizes and destroys twenty-one thousand Dianazene tablets from Distribution Center, Inc., due to false claims to cure radiation sickness.

1959: Hubbard Mark I E-Meter released, based on a version developed by early Dianetics enthusiast Volney Mathison.

Spring–Summer 1959: Hubbard purchases Saint Hill Manor (East Grinstead, United Kingdom), which becomes the international Scientology headquarters.

1960: Hubbard Mark II and Mark III E-Meters released.

April 30, 1960: David Miscavige born in Bucks County, Pennsylvania.

January 1961: Hubbard Mark IV E-Meter released.

March 1961–December 1966: Hubbard delivers over 400 lectures as part of the Saint Hill Special Briefing Course (SHSBC) in East Grinstead, United Kingdom.

January 4, 1963: Washington, DC, church raided by the US Marshals who were operating on a warrant from the FDA.

1965: Anderson Report published in Australia. It is followed by the Psychological Practices Act (1965), Scientology Act (1968), and Scientology Prohibition Act (1969), which effectively banned the practice of Scientology on the continent.

February 7, 1965: "Keeping Scientology Working: Series 1" (KSW), Hubbard's policy letter on orthopraxy, released.

May 5, 1965: "Classification, Gradation, and Awareness Chart," precursor to the current Bridge to Total Freedom, released in East Grinstead, United Kingdom.

September 1965: Clearing Course released at Saint Hill Manor (East Grinstead).

1966: John McMaster announced as the first true Clear.

1966: Helen O'Brien, Hubbard's former secretary and early Dianetics leader, publishes *Dianetics in Limbo*.

February 19, 1966: Narconon founded.

May 1966: Hubbard interviewed by Tony Hitchman for Rhodesian television.

August 1966: OT I released.

September 1966: OT II released.

September 1, 1966: Hubbard resigns as the executive director of international Scientology organizations.

August 12, 1967: Sea Organization (Sea Org) founded. Its precursor was the Sea Project. Hubbard and a dedicated small core of members transition to sea.

September 20, 1967: Hubbard announces release of OT III in audio recording *Ron's Journal 67*.

July 18, 1967: Church of Scientology of California (CSC) stripped of IRS tax-exempt status.

January 1968: OT IV, V, and VI released.

July 1968: Hubbard interviewed for "The Shrinking World of L. Ron Hubbard," produced by Granada TV.

August 1968: *Freedom* magazine founded by the Church of Scientology.

1968: *Ron's Journal 68* released.

1969: Standard Dianetics released.

1969: Citizens Commission on Human Rights (CCHR) founded in the United States (a separate organization was initially founded in 1968 in England).

1970: Criminon founded.

1970: Personal Spiritual Freedoms Foundation – later termed Dianology and then Eductivism – established by Jack Horner.

February 22, 1970: Church of Scientology Celebrity Centre (CC) founded in Los Angeles.

September 9, 1970: OT VII released.

November 1970: Hubbard begins delivery of Flag Executive Briefing Course (FEBC).

1970: *Scientology: The Now Religion* published by American journalist George Malko.

1971: Erhard Seminars Training (est) founded by Werner Erhard (now known as Landmark Education).

1971: *The Scandal of Scientology* published by American journalist Paulette Cooper.

1971: *The Mind Benders* published by British former member Cyril Vosper.

1971: *Ali's Smile: Naked Scientology* published by American author William S. Burroughs.

1971: Hubbard releases the L-Rundowns (L10, L11, and L12), now delivered at the Flag Land Base in Clearwater, Florida.

June 1972: *Inside Scientology: How I Joined Scientology and Became Superhuman* published by British former member Robert Kaufman.

August 18, 1972: Applied Scholastics founded.

1973: Scientology granted religious recognition in Australia.

1973: US Court of Appeals Judge Gerhard Gesell orders that E-Meters contain a disclaimer that the device offers no diagnostic or medical benefit.

1973–79: Guardian Office (GO) begins large-scale infiltration of governmental and professional offices, primarily in the United States. For her role in the GO's activities, Hubbard's wife Mary Sue Hubbard later served a year in prison. Several others plead guilty in connection with GO activities.

January 1974: Hubbard creates Rehabilitation Project Force (RPF) for the Sea Organization.

January 23, 1974: Introspection Rundown released.

October 1975: The Sea Org's Flag Service Organization transitions from sea to land, establishing temporary headquarters in Daytona Beach, Florida. In December 1975 the Flag Land Base is established in Clearwater, Florida. The name United Churches of Florida is employed to disguise connections to the Church of Scientology.

1976: *The Road to Total Freedom: A Sociological Analysis of Scientology* published by Roy Wallis.

July 8, 1977: United States Federal Bureau of Investigation (FBI) raids churches in Los Angeles and Washington, DC.

September 1977: Church acquires and establishes regional operations at former Cedars of Lebanon Medical Center in Los Angeles (now located at the corner of L. Ron Hubbard Way and Fountain Avenue).

1978: New Era Dianetics (NED) released.

September 1978: New OT V released (New Era Dianetics for OTs, or NOTS).

1978: Cult Awareness Network (CAN) founded by deprogrammer Ted Patrick.

March 1979: Hubbard Mark VI E-Meter released.

April 30, 1979: Watchdog Committee (WDC) established.

December 1979: Purification Rundown released. Its precursor was the "Sweat Program."

January 1980: New OT IV released (OT Drug Rundown).

February 1980: Senior Executive Strata established under the office of the Executive Director International.

August 1980: Golden Era Productions established. It is located in Gilman Hot Springs (Hemet), California, adjacent to international management headquarters.

September 1980: New OT VI (Hubbard Solo New Era Dianetics for Ots, or NOTS, Course) and OT VII (Solo NOTS auditing) released.

February 1981: *The Way to Happiness: A Common Sense Guide to Better Living* published.

November 1981: Mission Holders Conference in Clearwater, Florida.

November 19, 1981: Church of Scientology International (CSI), the ecclesiastical "Mother Church" of the Scientology religion, is founded. It replaces the Church of Scientology of California (CSC), founded in 1954.

December 22, 1981: Scientology Missions International (SMI) founded.

May 16, 1982: Religious Technology Center (RTC) incorporated. Hubbard donates Dianetics and Scientology trademarks to RTC.

May 27, 1982: Church of Spiritual Technology (CST) incorporated. CST owns Hubbard's copyrights and does business as the L. Ron Hubbard Library.

1982: Kenja Communication founded in Australia by Ken Dyers and Jan Hamilton.

1982: Hubbard's *Battlefield Earth* published.

October 1982: Mission Holders Conference in San Francisco.

1982: Field Auditor Conference anticipates the current International Hubbard Ecclesiastical League of Pastors (I HELP).

October 27, 1983: Australian High Court grants Scientology religious recognition.

December 1983: Office of Special Affairs International (OSAI) formed. OSAI coordinates public relations and legal affairs as part of the Church of Scientology International (CSI).

1983: Advanced Ability Center (AAC) founded by former Sea Org member David Mayo.

October 12, 1984: "Captain" Bill Robertson announces Ron's Org (Free Zone Scientology), now run by Max and Erica Hauri in Switzerland.

October 7, 1984: International Association of Scientologists (IAS) formed at Saint Hill Manor (East Grinstead). Attendees sign "Pledge to Mankind."

1985: Thousands of Scientologists participate in a Religious Freedom Crusade in Portland, Oregon, in connection to the Julie Christofferson court case.

October 1985: First of ten volumes (dekalogy) of Hubbard's *Mission Earth* released.

January 24, 1986: Hubbard dies ("drops the body") after suffering a stroke in Creston, California.

1986: The Avatar Course founded by Harry Palmer.

March 1987: David Miscavige becomes chairman of the board (COB) of the Religious Technology Center (RTC).

1987: *L. Ron Hubbard: Messiah or Madman?* published by Bent Corydon and Ronald DeWolf. DeWolf would later retract statements he made in the book and his name was removed from subsequent editions.

1987: BBC's *Panorama* produces documentary "Scientology: The Road to Total Freedom?"

1987: *Renunciation and Reformulation: A Study of Conversion in an American Sect* published by American anthropologist Harriet Whitehead (based on research conducted in preparation for her 1975 University of Chicago dissertation "What Does Scientology Auditing Do?").

June 6, 1988: Sea Organization motor vessel *Freewinds* christened in Curaçao. The following day, course rooms opened for the delivery of New OT VIII, the highest step currently available on the Bridge to Total Freedom.

November 14, 1988: Association for Better Living and Education (ABLE) incorporated in Los Angeles.

August 1990: *A Piece of Blue Sky: Scientology, Dianetics, and L. Ron Hubbard Exposed* published by British former member Jon Atack.

May 1991: Richard Behar publishes "Scientology: The Thriving Cult of Greed and Power" in *Time* magazine. The Church of Scientology later sued Time Warner for libel and the suit was dismissed in 1996.

July 1991: Online newsgroup *alt.religion.scientology* formed by Scott Charles Goehring.

September 7, 1991: Streamlined Bridge to Total Freedom (Grade Chart) released and remained in use until a new chart was released in November 2013 as part of the "Golden Age of Tech Phase II."

April 1993: "Fishman Affidavit" containing alleged portions of OT materials produced in federal case *Church of Scientology International v. Fishman and Geertz*.

October 1, 1993: Internal Revenue Service (IRS) in the United States grants tax-exempt status to all Church of Scientology and affiliated organizations. Soon after David Miscavige announces the news to ten thousand Scientologists at the Los Angeles Sports Arena in "The War is Over" event.

December 5, 1995: Scientologist Lisa McPherson dies in Clearwater, Florida. Critic Bob Minton later founded the Lisa McPherson Trust.

1996: Cult Awareness Network (CAN) driven to bankruptcy in wake of the Jason Scott case. The "Old CAN" would become the New Cult Awareness Network, operated by Scientologists. Files from the original organization are stored in Special Collections at the University of California, Santa Barbara Library (also home to the American Religions Collection donated by J. Gordon Melton).

May 10, 1996: "Golden Age of Technology" released, including new auditor training drills and the Hubbard Professional Mark Super VII Quantum E-Meter and Hubbard E-Meter Drills Simulator.

April 5, 1997: Street in Los Angeles near Scientology organizations renamed L. Ron Hubbard Way.

1999: "Rethinking Scientology: Cognition and Representation in Religion, Therapy, and Soteriology" written by the Danish religious historian Dorthe Refslund Christensen at the University of Aarhus (PhD dissertation).

1999: *Theology and Practice of a Contemporary Religion* published by the Church of Scientology International with international cooperation from religious studies scholars.

September 11, 2001: David Miscavige releases "The Wake-Up Call: The Urge of Planetary Clearing" after the 9/11 terrorist attacks in the United States. This leads to the creation of the "Ideal Org" program.

2005: Church of Scientology begins to open its L. Ron Hubbard Heritage Sites, which as of 2015 include restored landmarks in Bay Head, New Jersey; Phoenix, Arizona; Washington, DC; London; East Grinstead, UK; and Johannesburg, South Africa.

November 2005: Comedy Central television program *South Park* airs episode on Scientology and Tom Cruise entitled "Trapped in the Closet."

2007: BBC's *Panorama* produces documentary "Scientology and Me."

2007: Bridge Publications republishes Hubbard's classic books on Dianetics and Scientology, referred to by the Church of Scientology as the "Basics."

January 15, 2008: Tom Cruise video from International Association of Scientologists (IAS) event leaked to YouTube.

January 21, 2008: Online hacktivist group Anonymous releases "Message to Scientology" on YouTube.

2008–09: Anonymous carries out a series of international protests against the Church of Scientology as part of its "Project Chanology."

2009: *Scientology*, edited by James R. Lewis, published by Oxford University Press.

2010: *The Church of Scientology* published by J. Gordon Melton.

2010: BBC's *Panorama* produces documentary "The Secrets of Scientology."

August 2010: Hundreds of Nation of Islam (NOI) members participate in mass Dianetics seminar in Rosemont, Illinois. In July 2012 Louis Farrakhan stated: "Nobody can lead in our Nation until and unless they become Clear."

2011: *The Church of Scientology: A History of a New Religion* published by Hugh B. Urban. Urban subsequently donated research materials to create a Scientology special collection at Ohio State University.

2011: *Inside Scientology: The Story of America's Most Secretive Religion* published by American journalist Janet Reitman.

2011: Lawrence Wright publishes "The Apostate," based on an interview with filmmaker and former Scientologist Paul Haggis, in *The New Yorker*.

December 31, 2011: Debbie Cook, former Sea Org executive at the Flag Land Base in Clearwater, Florida, sends an email to thousands of Scientologists outlining grievances with church management.

July 2012: Dror Center (Israel) defects from the Church of Scientology International and establishes an independent Scientology center run by Dani and Tami Lemberger.

2012: Kate Bornstein publishes *A Queer and Pleasant Danger*.

2012: Bridge Publications publishes sixteen-volume L. Ron Hubbard Series: The Complete Biographical Encyclopedia.

September 2012: Film *The Master*, directed by Paul Thomas Anderson, released.

Late 2012: Journalist Tony Ortega leaves the *Village Voice* and maintains a daily blog on Scientology and other topics entitled "The Underground Bunker."

2013: *Going Clear: Scientology, Hollywood, and the Prison of Belief* published by American journalist Lawrence Wright.

November 2013: Mark Ultra VIII E-Meter released.

November 2013: Flag "Super Power" Building opened in Clearwater, Florida, to accommodate release of Super Power Rundowns and Cause Resurgence Rundown.

January 2014: International academic conference on Scientology held in Antwerp, Belgium, and sponsored by the Faculty for the Comparative Study of Religion (FVG).

March 2015: Documentary "Going Clear: Scientology and the Prison of Belief," directed by American Alex Gibney, released. Based on the 2013 book by the American journalist Lawrence Wright.

May 2015: "A People's History of the Church of Scientology" written by Donald A. Westbrook at Claremont Graduate University (unpublished PhD dissertation). Westbrook donates research materials to the Claremont Colleges Library.

June 2015: James Beverley and Jon Atack organize "Getting Clear" conference in Toronto, Canada.

October 2015: *My Scientology Movie*, directed by John Dower and featuring Louis Theroux, released.

2017: *Handbook of Scientology* published by coeditors James R. Lewis and Kjersti Hellesøy.

2017: *Scientology in Popular Culture: Influences and Struggles for Legitimacy* published by coeditors Stephen A. Kent and Susan Raine.

Fall 2017: Grand opening of the Edward E. Marsh Golden Age of Science Fiction Reading Room at San Diego State University's Special Collections and University Archives.

March 2018: Scientology TV launched.

March–April 2018: *Journal of CESNUR*, inaugurated the previous year, publishes a special issue on Scientology.

December 2018: *Among the Scientologists: History, Theology, and Praxis* published by Donald A. Westbrook.

December 2018: "Auditing in Contemporary Scientologies: The Self, Authenticity, and Material Culture" dissertation completed by Aled Thomas. Dr. Thomas later publishes *Free Zone Scientology: Contesting the Boundaries of a New Religion* (April 2021).

2020: Church of Scientology International (CSI) launches "Stay Well" and other humanitarian campaigns in response to the COVID-19 pandemic.

March 2022: "Golden Age of Admin" (Administration) announced.

Appendix B
Selected Archives and Finding Aids

American Religions Collection. University of California, Santa Barbara, Special Collections. Online Archive of California (OAC) finding aid: https://oac.cdlib .org/findaid/ark:/13030/tf3779n92n/

Church of Scientology Collection (1133) and Louis Jolyon West Papers (LSC.0590). Charles E. Young Research Library. University of California, Los Angeles, Special Collections. Online Archive of California (OAC) finding aids: https://oac.cdlib.org/findaid/ark:/13030/kt4580212s/ and https://oac.cdlib.org/ findaid/ark:/13030/c84j0hcd/

Edward E. Marsh Ephemera Collection. San Diego State University Special Collections. Online Archive of California (OAC) finding aid: https://oac.cdlib .org/findaid/ark:/13030/c85q51mp/

Hugh B. Urban Scientology Collection. Ohio State University Special Collections. Finding aid: https://library.osu.edu/finding-aids//ead/RARE/SPEC.RARE .CMS.0382.xml

Robert Vaughn Young Memorial Scientology Collection. Graduate Theological Union Special Collections, Berkeley, California. http://tinyurl.com/yxgrred4

Stephen A. Kent Collection on Alternative Beliefs (Restricted Collection). University of Alberta Library, Canada. https://apps.ualberta.ca/directory/ person/skent

Westbrook Scientology Collection. Claremont Colleges Library, Special Collections. Claremont, California. Online Archive of California (OAC) finding aid: https://oac.cdlib.org/findaid/ark:/13030/c8765kwb/

Bibliography

Bainbridge, W. (1987). Science and Religion: The Case of Scientology. In D. G. Bromley & P. E. Hammond (eds.), *The Future of New Religious Movements* (59–79). Macon, GA: Mercer University Press.

Bainbridge, W., & Stark, R. (1980). Scientology: To Be Perfectly Clear. *Sociological Analysis*, *41*(2), 128–36.

Bigliardi, S. (2017). Earth as Battlefield and Mission: Knowledge, Technology, and Power in LR Hubbard's Late Novels. In S. A. Kent & S. Raine (eds.), *Scientology in Popular Culture: Influences and Struggles for Legitimacy* (53–80). Santa Barbara, CA: ABC-CLIO.

Camacho, I. C. (2020). Degrees of "Truthiness": A Response to Stephen A. Kent. *Journal of CESNUR*. Supplement to *3*(1). https://doi.org/10.26338/tjoc.2020.suppbis.3.1

Chagnon, R. (1985). *La Scientologie: une nouvelle religion de la puissance.* Villa de LaSalle, Québec: Hurtubise HMH.

Christensen, D. R. (1999). Rethinking Scientology: Cognition and Representation in Religion, Therapy and Soteriology (PhD dissertation). University of Aarhus.

Christensen, D. R. (2005). Inventing L. Ron Hubbard: On the Construction and Maintenance of the Hagiographic Mythology of Scientology's Founder. In J. R. Lewis (ed.), *Controversial New Religions* (227–58). New York: Oxford University Press.

Christensen, D. R. (2009). Sources for the Study of Scientology: Presentations and Reflections. In J. R. Lewis (ed.), *Scientology* (411–31). New York: Oxford University Press.

Christensen, D. R. (2017). Rethinking Scientology: An Analysis of L. Ron Hubbard's Formulation of Therapy and Religion in Dianetics and Scientology, 1950–1986. In J. R. Lewis & K. Hellesøy (eds.), *Handbook of Scientology* (47–103). Leiden: Brill.

Church of Scientology Flag Service Organization (2010). 10,000 on SOLO NOTs: An OT Boom of Unimaginable Proportions. Pamphlet.

Church of Scientology Flag Service Organization (2021). Be One of the First 10,000 on SOLO NOTs. *FSM Newsletter*, Issue 67.

Church of Scientology International (1982). The Flow Up the Bridge: The US Mission Holders Conference, San Francisco 1982. Sea Organization Executive Directive Number 2104, November 7.

Church of Scientology International (1988). *The Command Channels of Scientology*. Los Angeles: Bridge.

Church of Scientology International (1998). *What Is Scientology?* Los Angeles: Bridge. www.whatisscientology.org/html/Part02/Chp06/pg0181_1.html

Church of Scientology International (1999). *Scientology: Theology and Practice of a Contemporary Religion.* Los Angeles: Bridge.

Church of Scientology International (2011). Defrocked Apostates: The Road to Redemption. *Freedom.* www.freedommag.org/special-reports/sources/defrocked-apostates-the-road-to-redemption.html

Church of Scientology International (2014). *Walk in Ron's Footsteps: L. Ron Hubbard Landmark Sites.* Los Angeles: Bridge.

Church of Scientology International (2019). Winds of Change: Scientology Headquarters for Africa Springs to Life at Majestic Castle Kyalami. www.scientology.org/scientology-today/church-openings/grand-opening-advanced-org-saint-hill-africa.html

Church of Scientology International (2021a). Meet a Scientologist. www.scientologynews.org/press-releases/meet-scientologists

Church of Scientology International (2021b). The Technology of Study. Online Course. www.scientology.org/courses/study/overview.html

Church of Scientology International (2021c). L. Ron Hubbard Landmark Sites. www.lronhubbard.org/landmark-sites

Church of Scientology International (2021d). Find Your Nearest Scientology Organization. www.scientology.org/churches/locator.html

Church of Scientology International (2021e). Welcome to the *Freewinds.* www.freewinds.org

Church of Scientology International (2021f). How We Help. www.scientology.org/how-we-help

Church of Scientology International (2021g). Organizing Board. www.scientologycourses.org/tools-for-life/organizing/steps/organizing-board.html

Church of Scientology International (2021h). David Miscavige, Chairman of the Board, Religious Technology Center & Ecclesiastical Leader of the Scientology Religion. www.scientology.org/david-miscavige

Church of Scientology International (2021i). Scientology TV. www.scientology.tv

Church of Scientology International (2022). David Miscavige: Chairman of the Board, Religious Technology Center, and Ecclesiastical Leader of the Scientology Religion. www.davidmiscavige.org/about

Church of Scientology Religious Trust (2021). L. Ron Hubbard Hall, *Expansion Magazine* Issue 26. Following Ron's Adventures.

Citizens Commission on Human Rights (2021). What Is the Citizens Commission on Human Rights (CCHR)? www.cchr.org/about-us/what-is-cchr.html

Cowan, D. E. (2009). Researching Scientology: Perceptions, Premises, Promises, and Problematics. In J. R. Lewis (ed.), *Scientology* (53–79). New York: Oxford University Press.

Cusack, C. M. (2017). "Squirrels" and Unauthorized Uses of Scientology: Werner Erhard and est, Ken Dyers and Kenja, and Harvey Jackins and Re-evaluation Counselling. In J. R. Lewis & K. Hellesøy (eds.), *Handbook of Scientology* (485–506). Leiden: Brill.

Cusack, C. M. (2020). Apostate Memoirs and the Study of Scientology in the Twenty-First Century. *Implicit Religion, 23*(2), 148–55.

Dallam, M. W. (2011). Ethical Problems in New Religion Field Research. *Religion Compass, 5*(9), 528–35.

Dericquebourg, R. (2010). Legitimizing Belief through the Authority of Science: The Case of the Church of Scientology. In J. R. Lewis & O. Hammer (eds.), *Handbook of Religion and the Authority of Science* (741–62). Leiden: Brill.

Dericquebourg, R. (2017a). Scientology: From the Edges to the Core. *Nova Religio, 20*(4), 5–12.

Dericquebourg, R. (2017b). Affinities between Scientology and Theosophy. *Acta Comparanda*, Subsidia IV: 81–103.

Doherty, B. (2013). Sensational Scientology! The Church of Scientology and Australian Tabloid Television. *Nova Religio, 17*(3), 38–63. https://doi.org/10.1525/nr.2014.17.3.38

Doherty, B. (2017). The Anderson Inquiry and Its Australian aftermath. In J. R. Lewis & K. Hellesøy (eds.), *Handbook of Scientology* (249–78). Leiden: Brill.

Doherty, B. (2019). New Directions in the Study of Scientology: A View from the Academy. The Religious Studies Podcast. www.religiousstudiesproject.com/response/new-directions-in-the-study-of-scientology-a-view-from-the-academy ·

Doherty, B. (2020). Handle with Care: Reflections on the Academic Study of Scientology. *Implicit Religion, 23*(2), 102–28.

Doherty, B., & Richardson, J. T. (2019). Litigation, Liberty, and Legitimation: The Experience of the Church of Scientology in Australian Law. *St. Mark's Review, 247*, 61–81.

Fischer, H. J. (1953). Dianetic Therapy: An Experimental Evaluation: A Statistical Analysis of the Effect of Dianetic Therapy as Measured by Group Tests of Intelligence, Mathematics and Personality. PhD dissertation. New York: New York University.

Flinn, F. K. (2009). Scientology as Technological Buddhism. In J. R. Lewis (ed.), *Scientology* (209–24). New York: Oxford University Press.

Fox, J., Davis, A. E. & Lebovits, B. (1959). An Experimental Investigation of Hubbard's Engram Hypothesis (Dianetics). *Psychological Newsletter, 10*, 131–34.

Frenschkowski, M. (2010). Researching Scientology: Some Observations on Recent Literature, English and German. *Alternative Spirituality and Religion Review, 1*(1), 5–44.

Frenschkowski, M. (2017). Images of Religions and Religious History in the Works of L. Ron Hubbard. In J. R. Lewis & K. Hellesøy (eds.), *Handbook of Scientology* (104–40). Leiden: Brill.

Golden Era Productions. (2006). *Introduction to Scientology.* Los Angeles, L. Ron Hubbard interview conducted by Scientologist Tony Hitchman, 1966.

Graham, R. (2014, November 5). Are Academics Afraid to Study Scientology? (originally published as The Scholarly Study of Scientology). *JSTOR Daily.* https://daily.jstor.org/scholars-on-scientology

Granada Television. (1968, August). The Shrinking World of L. Ron Hubbard. *World in Action.* https://youtu.be/L_w-YWwC1lI

Gregg, S. E. (2020). Researching and Teaching Scientology: Perception and Performance of a New Religion. *Implicit Religion, 23*(2), 129–39.

Gregg, S. E., & A. J. L. Thomas. (2019). Scientology Inside Out: Complex Religious Belonging in the Church of Scientology and the Free Zone. In G. D. Chryssides and S. E. Gregg (eds.), *The Insider/Outsider Debate: New Perspectives in the Study of Religion* (350–70). Sheffield: Equinox.

Grünschloß, A. (2009). Scientology, a "New Age" Religion? In J. R. Lewis (ed.), *Scientology* (225–43). New York: Oxford University Press.

Guinness World Records. (2022). Most Published Works by One Author [L. Ron Hubbard]. www.guinnessworldrecords.com/world-records/most-published-works-by-one-author

Hellesøy, K. (2015). Independent Scientology: How Ron's Org and Dror Center Schismed out of the Church of Scientology (MA thesis). Arctic University of Norway. https://munin.uit.no/handle/10037/8353

Hubbard College of Administration International. (2020). Pattern of the Organization. https://web.archive.org/web/20200512090707/https://hubbard college.org/administrative-technology.php

Hubbard, L. R. (1950a). Dianetics: The Evolution of a Science. *Astounding Science Fiction.* May issue.

Hubbard, L. R. (1950b). *Terra Incognita*: The Mind. *The Explorers Journal.* Winter–Spring issue.

Hubbard, L. R. (1958). Signs of Success. Hubbard Communications Office Policy Letter. May 1.

Hubbard, L. R. (1959a). HCO WW Changes Quarters and Address. Hubbard Communications Office. June 26.

Hubbard, L. R. (1959b). Special Information for Mission Holders. Hubbard Communications Office Bulletin. July 14.

Hubbard, L. R. (1959c). News Bulletin. Hubbard Communications Office Bulletin. September 14.

Hubbard, L. R. (1961). Personal Integrity. *Ability*, Issue 125. [Republished in *Scientology: A New Slant on Life*, 19. Los Angeles: Bridge, 2007].

Hubbard, L. R. (1965). Keeping Scientology Working Series 1. Hubbard Communications Office Policy Letter, February 7.

Hubbard, L. R. (1971a). Opinion Leaders. Hubbard Communications Office Policy Letter. May 11.

Hubbard, L. R. (1971b.) Welcome to the Flag Intern Course. Lecture given on June 12, 1971.

Hubbard, L. R. (1972). How to Handle Black Propaganda. Hubbard Communications Office Policy Letter. November 21.

Hubbard, L. R. (1974). *Hymn of Asia*. Los Angeles: Bridge.

Hubbard, L. R. (1975). *Dianetics and Scientology Technical Dictionary*. Los Angeles: Publications Organization.

Hubbard, L. R. (1982a). The Safe Point. Hubbard Communications Office Policy Letter. April 1.

Hubbard, L. R. (1982b). *Battlefield Earth: A Saga of the Year 3000*. New York: St. Martin's.

Hubbard, L. R. (1982c). Revision of the Birthday Game 1982/83. Executive Directive 339 R, March 13, 1982, revised July 30, 1982.

Hubbard, L. R. (1985–87). *Mission Earth*. 10 volumes ("dekalogy"). Republished by Los Angeles: Galaxy Press.

Hubbard, L. R. (1989). *Have You Lived Before This Life?* Los Angeles: Bridge.

Hubbard L. R. (1990). *Clear Body, Clear Mind*. Los Angeles: Bridge.

Hubbard, L. R. (1997). The Role of Earth. Lecture delivered November 1952 [transcript]. Research and Discovery Series, vol. 12. Los Angeles: Bridge.

Hubbard, L. R. (2005). *Ron's Journal 67*. Los Angeles: Golden Era Productions.

Hubbard, L. R. (2007a). Policies on Physical Healing: Insanity and 'Sources of Trouble.' In L. R. Hubbard, *Introduction to Scientology Ethics* (216–22). Los Angeles: Bridge.

Hubbard, L. R. (2007b). *Self Analysis*. Los Angeles: Bridge.

Hubbard, L. R. (2007c). *Scientology: The Fundamentals of Thought*. Los Angeles: Bridge.

Hubbard, L. R. (2007d). *Dianetics: The Evolution of a Science*. Los Angeles: Bridge.

Hubbard, L. R. (2007e). *Dianetics: The Original Thesis*. Los Angeles: Bridge.

Hubbard, L. R. (2007f). *Dianetics: The Modern Science of Mental Health*. Los Angeles: Bridge.

Hubbard, L. R. (2007g). From Clear to Eternity. In L. Ron Hubbard, *Scientology 0–8: The Book of Basics* (430–33). Los Angeles: Bridge.

Hubbard, L. R. (2007h). *The Phoenix Lectures*. Los Angeles: Golden Era Productions.

Hubbard, L. R. (2007i). *The Creation of Human Ability: A Handbook for Scientologists*. Los Angeles: Bridge.

Hubbard, L. R. (2007j). *The Way to Happiness: A Common Sense Guide to Better Living*. Los Angeles: Bridge.

Hubbard, L. R. (2007k). *Scientology: A History of Man*. Los Angeles: Bridge.

Hubbard, L. R. (2008). Classification and Gradation. *Lecture given on September 9, 1965*. Los Angeles: Golden Era Productions.

Hubbard, L. R. (2009a). *The Free Being*. Los Angeles: Golden Era Productions.

Hubbard, L. R. (2009b). *State of Man Congress*. Los Angeles: Golden Era Productions.

Hubbard, L. R. (2009c). Radiation and Scientology. Lecture given on April 13, 1957. *London Congress on Nuclear Radiation, Control, and Health*. Los Angeles: Golden Era Productions.

Hubbard, L. R. (2009d). The Goals Problem Mass. Lecture given on December 31, 1961. *Clean Hands Congress*. Los Angeles: Golden Era Productions.

Hubbard, L. R. (2010). *Philadelphia Doctorate Course*. Los Angeles: Golden Era Productions.

Hubbard, L. R. (2012a). L. Ron Hubbard Discusses the Development of His Philosophy. Interview with J. Stillson Judah. In *Philosopher and Founder: Rediscovery of the Human Soul* (87–91). Los Angeles: Bridge.

Hubbard, L. R. (2012b). My Only Defense for Having Lived. In *Philosopher and Founder: Rediscovery of the Human Soul* (137–45). Los Angeles: Bridge.

Hubbard, L. R. (2012c). *Dianetics: Letters and Journals*. Los Angeles: Bridge.

Hubbard, L. R. (2012d). My Philosophy. In *Philosopher and Founder: Rediscovery of the Human Soul*. Los Angeles: Bridge.

Ibanez, D., Southon, G., Southon, P. & Benton, P. (1951). *Dianetic Processing: A Brief Survey of Research Projects and Preliminary Results*. Elizabeth, NJ: Hubbard Dianetic Research Foundation.

Introvigne, M. (2017a). The Aesthetic Theory of L. Ron Hubbard and the *Freewinds* as a Mobile Holy Land. Center for Studies on New Religions (CESNUR). www.cesnur.org/2017/jer_mi_scientology.pdf

Introvigne, M. (2017b). Reza Aslan on Scientology: Much Ado about Not Very Much? Center for Studies on New Religions (CESNUR). www.cesnur.org/2017/reza_aslan.htm

Introvigne, M. (2017c). Did L. Ron Hubbard Believe in Brainwashing? The Strange Story of the "Brain-Washing Manual" of 1955. *Nova Religio, 20*(4), 62–79. https://doi.org/10.1525/nr.2017.20.4.62

Introvigne, M. (2017d). Scientology: Genesis, Exodus, and Numbers: Fake News about Scientology Statistics. Center for Studies on New Religions (CESNUR). www.cesnur.org/2017/scientology_numbers.htm

Introvigne, M. (2018a, November 18). Even Scientology Can Be Studied: Gordon Melton and the Wisdom of Diversity. American Academy of Religion Annual Meeting, Denver, Colorado. www.cesnur.org/2018/melton_scientology_denver.pdf

Introvigne, M. (2018b). "The Most Misunderstood Human Endeavor": L. Ron Hubbard, Scientology, and the Fine Arts. *Journal of CESNUR, 2*(2), 60–92. https://doi.org/10.26338/tjoc.2018.2.2.4

Introvigne, M. (2019). The Gnostic L. Ron Hubbard: Was He Influenced by Aleister Crowley? *Journal of CESNUR, 3*(3), 53–81. https://doi.org/10.26338/tjoc.2019.3.3.3

Introvigne, M. (2020). Scientology Studies 2.0, Utopia or Opportunity? *Implicit Religion, 23*(2), 156–66.

Johnson, C. J. (1984). Cancer Incidence in an Area of Radioactive Fallout Downwind from the Nevada Test Site. *Journal of the American Medical Association, 251*(2), 230–36.

Jones, J. M. (2008, April 15). Americans have Net-Positive view of US Catholics. Gallup. www.gallup.com/poll/106516/Americans-NetPositive-View-US-Catholics.aspx

Judah, J. S. (1975). Garden Conversation with the Chairman of the Religion Dept. of USC, and Dr. Stillson Judah, and Others. June 24. https://vanisource.org/wiki/750624_-_Conversation_-_Los_Angeles

Kaplan, J. (2006). New Religious Movements and Globalization. In E. V. Gallagher & W. M. Ashcraft (eds.), *Introduction to New and Alternative Religions in America*, vol. 1 (84–125). Westport, CT: Greenwood Press.

Kent, S. A. (1996). Scientology's Relationship with Eastern Religious Traditions. *Journal of Contemporary Religion 11*(1), 21–36.

Kent, S. A. (1999). The Creation of "Religious" Scientology. *Religious Studies and Theology, 18*, 97–126. https://doi.org/10.1558/rsth.v18i2.97

Kent, S. A. (2020). Degrees of Embellishment: Scientology, L. Ron Hubbard, and His Civil Engineering Credentials Fraud. *Journal of CESNUR.* Supplement to *3*(1), vi–lx. https://doi.org/10.26338/tjoc.2020.supp.3.1

Kent, S. A., & Raine, S. (eds.) (2017). *Scientology in Popular Culture: Influences and Struggles for Legitimacy.* Santa Barbara, CA: ABC-CLIO.

Lewis, J. R. (1999). Let the Scholar Who is Without Sin Cast the First Stone. *Skeptic*, *7*(1), 18–21. www.skeptic.com/magazine/archives/7.1/

Lewis, J. R. (ed.). (2009). *Scientology.* New York: Oxford University Press.

Lewis, J. R. (2010). The Science Canopy: Religion, Legitimacy, and the Charisma of Science. *Temenos: Nordic Journal of Comparative Religion*, *46*(1), 7–29.

Lewis, J. R. (2013). Free Zone Scientology and Other Movement Milieus: A Preliminary Characterization. *Temenos*, *49*, 255–76.

Lewis, J. R. (2015). Scientology: Sect, Science, or Scam? *Numen*, *62*, 226–42.

Lewis, J. R., & Hellesøy, K. (eds.). (2017). *Handbook of Scientology.* Leiden: Brill.

Lord, P. (2019). Scientology's Legal System. *Marburg Journal of Religion*, *21*(1), 1–34.

Melton, J. G. (1999). Mea Culpa! Mea Culpa! *Skeptic*, *7*(1), 14–17. www.skeptic.com/magazine/archives/7.1

Melton, J. G. (2000). *The Church of Scientology.* Salt Lake City: Signature Books.

Melton, J. G. (2009). Birth of a Religion. In J. R. Lewis (ed.), *Scientology* (17–33). New York: Oxford University Press.

Melton, J. G. (2017). On Doing Research on Scientology: Prospects and Pitfalls. *Acta Comparanda*, Subsidia IV, 11–20.

Melton, J. G. (2018). A Contemporary Ordered Religious Community: The Sea Organization. *Journal of CESNUR*, *2*(2), 21–59.

Miller, R. (2014). *Bare-Faced Messiah: The True Story of L. Ron Hubbard.* [Originally published in 1987 by Penguin.] London: Silvertail Books.

Miscavige, D. (2001, September 11). Wake-Up Call: The Urgency of Planetary Clearing. *Inspector General Network Bulletin, 44.* Religious Technology Center.

Muhammad, L. (2017). Leo Muhammad: Auditing, Dianetics & Scientology. YouTube. February 28. www.youtube.com/watch?v=kNM1azd4UEw

Muhammad, A. M. (2013, February 28). Nation of Islam Auditors Graduation Held for Third Saviours' Day in a Row. *Final Call.* www.finalcall.com/artman/publish/National_News_2/article_9651.shtml

Nevala-Lee, A. (2018). *Astounding: John W. Campbell, Isaac Asimov, Robert A. Heinlein, L. Ron Hubbard, and the Golden Age of Science Fiction.* New York: HarperCollins.

O'Brien, H. (1966). *Dianetics in Limbo: A Documentary about Immortality.* Philadelphia: Whitmore.

Old Timers Network. (2000). *LRH Stories* and *More LRH Stories*. Two-DVD Set. Self-published, 1997–2000. https://web.archive.org/web/20200130 205638/http://lrhstories.org

Parenti, C. (2021, November 18). The First Privilege Walk. Nonsite.org. https:// nonsite.org/the-first-privilege-walk/#

Possamai, A., & Possamai-Inesedy, A. (2012). Battlefield Earth and Scientology: A Cultural/Religious Industry à la Frankfurt School? In C. Cusack & A. Norman (eds.), *Handbook of New Religions and Cultural Production* (583–98). Leiden: Brill.

Raine, S. (2017). Colonizing *Terra Incognita*: L. Ron Hubbard, Scientology, and the Quest for Empire. In S. A. Kent & S. Raine (eds.), *Scientology in Popular Culture: Influence and Struggles for Legitimacy* (1–32). Santa Barbara, CA: Praeger.

Rathbun, M. (2013). *Memoirs of a Scientology Warrior*. Self-published: Amazon Books.

Reitman, J. (2011). *Inside Scientology: The Story of America's Most Secretive Religion*. New York: Mariner Books.

Religious Studies Podcast. (2018). New Directions in the Study of Scientology. Podcast episode featuring Aled Thomas, Stephen Gregg, Carole Cusack, and David G. Robertson. www.religiousstudiesproject.com/podcast/new-direc tions-in-the-study-of-scientology

Rigal-Cellard, B. (2009). Scientology Missions International (SMI): An Immutable Model of Technological Missionary Activity. In J. R. Lewis (ed.), *Scientology* (325–34). New York: Oxford University Press.

Rigal-Cellard, B. (2019). The Visible Expansion of the Church of Scientology and Its Actors. *Journal of CESNUR*, *3*(1), 8–118.

Rigal-Cellard, B. (2020). "Do Not Dare Speak of Scientology in France!" *Implicit Religion*, *23*(2), 182–92.

Rothstein, M. (2014). Emblematic Architecture and the Routinization of Charisma in Scientology. *International Journal for the Study of New Religions*, *5*(1), 51–74.

Rothstein, M. (2017). Space, Place and Religious Hardware: L. Ron Hubbard's Charismatic Authority in the Church of Scientology. In J. R. Lewis & K. Hellesøy (eds.), *Handbook of Scientology* (509–35). Leiden: Brill.

Roux, E. (2017). Scientology: From Controversy to Global Expansion and Recognition. In E. V. Gallagher (ed.), *"Cult Wars" in Historical Perspective: New and Minority Religions* (165–76). New York: Routledge.

Roux, E. (2018a). Scientology Auditing: Pastoral Counselling or a Religious Path to Total Spiritual Freedom. In S. Harvey, S. Steidinger & J. A. Beckford (eds.), *New Religious Movements and Counselling: Academic, Professional and Personal Perspectives* (130–42). New York: Routledge.

Roux, E. (2018b). *Sur la Scientologie*. Paris: Éditions Pierre-Guillaume de Roux.

Roux, E. (2020). Academic Study of Scientology: The Scientology Perspective. *Implicit Religion*, 23(2), 175–81.

Roux, E. (2021). Scientology behind the Scenes: The Law Changer. In E. Barker & J. T. Richardson (eds.), *Reactions to the Law by Minority Religions* (58–78). New York: Routledge.

San Diego State University. (2022). Perennial Wisdom Resources. SDSU Special Collections. https://library.sdsu.edu/scua/new-notable/perennial-wis dom-resources-theosophy-western-esotericism-and-essential-unity-all

Scientology Parent. (2021). www.scientologyparent.com

Shugart, C. (2018). *Fractured Journey: A Personal Account of 30 Outrageous Years in the Church of Scientology*. Self-published: Shugart Media.

Šorytė, R. (2020). "We Can Lift This World While Quarantined": Scientology and the 2020 Pandemic. *Journal of CESNUR*, 4(4), 3–24.

STAND League. (2019). Stephen Kent. Scientologists Taking Action Against Discrimination (STAND) League. www.standleague.org/bigotry-and-hate/ exposed/stephen-kent.html

STAND League. (2021). The "Snow White" Program and the Church of Scientology: The True Story. Scientologists Taking Action Against Discrimination (STAND) League. www.standleague.org/resources/whitepa pers/the-snow-white-program-and-the-church-of-scientology-the-true-story .html

Sterling, D. L. (1952). *Sex in the Basic Personality*. Wichita, KS: Hubbard Dianetic Foundation.

Stuckrad, K.von. (2014). *The Scientification of Religion: An Historical Study of Discursive Change, 1800–2000*. Boston: De Gruyter.

Terrin, A. N. (2017a). *Scientology: Libertà e immortalità*. Brescia: Morcelliana.

Terrin, A. N. (2017b). Scientology and Its Contiguity with Gnostic Religion and Eastern Religions. *Acta Comparanda*, Subsidia IV, 185–203.

Thomas, A. (2019). *Auditing in Contemporary Scientologies: The Self, Authenticity, and Material Culture* (PhD thesis). Open University. http:// oro.open.ac.uk/61691

Thomas, A. (2020). Engaging with the Church of Scientology and the Free Zone in the Field: Challenges, Barriers, and Methods. *International Journal for the Study of New Religions*, published online November 25, 2020. https://doi .org/10.1558/ijsnr.41396

Thomas, A. (2021). *Free Zone Scientology: Contesting the Boundaries of a New Religion*. London: Bloomsbury.

Tilden, F. (2008). *Interpreting Our Heritage*. 4th rev. ed. Chapel Hill: University of North Carolina Press.

Urban, H. B. (2010, March 18). The Rundown Truth: Scientology Changes Strategy in War with Media. *Religion Dispatches*. http://religiondispatches .org/the-rundown-truth-scientology-changes-strategy-in-war-with-media

Urban, H. B. (2011). *The Church of Scientology: A History of a New Religion*. Princeton, NJ: Princeton University Press.

Urban, H. B. (2012). The Occult Roots of Scientology? L. Ron Hubbard, Aleister Crowley, and the Origins of a Controversial Religion. *Nova Religio*, *15*(3), 91–116.

Urban, H. B. (2017). "The Third Wall of Fire": Scientology and the Study of Religious Secrecy. *Nova Religio*, *20*(4), 13–36.

Urban, H. B. (2019). The Knowing of Knowing: Neo-Gnosticism from the O.T. O. to Scientology. *Gnosis: Journal of Gnostic Studies*, *4*, 99–116.

van Vogt, A. E. (1964). *Reflections of A.E. van Vogt*. Transcript based on 1961 interview conducted by Elizabeth I. Dixon. UCLA Library Special Collections, Oral History Program.

Wallis, R. (1975). Scientology: Therapeutic Cult to Religious Sect. *Sociology*, *9*(1), 89–100. https://doi.org/10.1177/003803857500900105

Wallis, R. (1976). *The Road to Total Freedom: A Sociological Analysis of Scientology*. London: Heinemann. Republished in 1977 by New York: Columbia University Press.

Wallis, R. (1977). The Moral Career of a Research Project. In C. Bell & H. Newby (eds.), *Doing Sociological Research*. New York: Free Press.

Ward, D. J. (2014). Fair Sailing. *Freedom*. December 2014 Special Edition. Retrieved from www.freedommag.org/issue/201412-expansion/fair-sailing .html

Westbrook, D. A. (2015). Saint Hill and the Development of Systematic Theology in the Church of Scientology, 1959-1967. *Alternative Spirituality and Religion Review*, *6*(1), 111–55.

Westbrook, D. A. (2016). Walking in Ron's Footsteps: "Pilgrimage" Sites of the Church of Scientology. *Numen*, *63*, 71–94.

Westbrook, D. A. (2017a). Researching Scientology and Scientologists in the United States: Methods and Conclusions. In J. R. Lewis & K. Hellesøy (eds.), *Handbook of Scientology* (19–46). Leiden: Brill.

Westbrook, D. A. (2017b). The L. Ron Hubbard Heritage Site in Bay Head, New Jersey As a Case Study of Scientology's Intellectual History. *Acta Comparanda*, Subsidia IV, 225–42.

Westbrook, D. A. (2017c). "The Enemy of My Enemy Is My Friend": Thomas Szasz, the Citizens Commission on Human Rights, and Scientology's Anti-Psychiatric Theology. *Nova Religio, 20*(4), 37–61.

Westbrook, D. A. (2018). The Art of PR War: Scientology, the Media, and Legitimation Strategies for the 21st Century. *Studies in Religion/Sciences Religeuses, 47*, 373–95.

Westbrook, D. A. (2019). *Among the Scientologists: History, Theology, and Praxis*. New York: Oxford University Press.

Westbrook, D. A. (2020). Scientology Studies 2.0: Lessons Learned and Paths Forward. *Religion Compass, 14*(2), 1–11.

Westbrook, D. A., & Lewis, J. R. (2019). Scientology and Gnosticism: L. Ron Hubbard's "The Factors." In G. W. Trompf, G. B. Mikkelsen, & J. Johnston (eds.), *The Gnostic World* (632–37). London: Routledge.

Whitehead, H. (1975). *What Does Scientology Auditing do?* (PhD dissertation). University of Chicago.

Whitehead, H. (1987). *Renunciation and Reformulation: A Study of Conversion in an American Sect*. Ithaca, NY: Cornell University Press.

Winter, J. A. (1951). *A Doctor's Report on Dianetics*. New York: Julian Press.

Wolfe, J. H. (2017). Common Sense Scientology. *Humanistic Psychologist, 45*, 84–97.

Wolfe, J. H. (2021). Personality Testing in the Church of Scientology: Implications for Outcome Research. *SSRN*. https://ssrn.com/abstract=2980160.

Wright, L. (2013). *Going Clear: Scientology, Hollywood, and the Prison of Belief*. New York: Knopf.

Acknowledgments

This work would not have been possible without support from San Diego State University, where I was based as a postdoctoral research fellow during the 2019–20 academic year. A number of important archival centers of Scientology studies now exist in North America, but the collections in San Diego are truly exceptional for their breadth and depth. Equally important, the university continues to make these materials available to both researchers and the general public. In turn, SDSU owes an immeasurable debt to Edward E. Marsh, who has donated large portions of his significant Scientology and SF collection to the university and maintains an impressive private library of his own. For many years, the Marsh Collections at SDSU were overseen by the inimitable Robert Ray, the retired head of special collections and now an emeritus librarian, who brought to bear considerable research expertise and an appreciation for the study of new and alternative religious traditions. I am grateful to both Ed and Rob for their support of this project and for "getting" my approach to the life and legacy of L. Ron Hubbard.

Numerous Scientologists – both inside and outside the Sea Organization (the Church of Scientology's priestly organization), including friends I made before, during, and after writing my first book, *Among the Scientologists* – offered support and directed me to sources. I am particularly thankful for feedback from Lynn Farny and Jason Medeiros.

This and my larger work on Scientology rests on the shoulders of giants in the study of new religions, such as Roy Wallis, Harriet Whitehead, J. Gordon Melton, James R. Lewis, Massimo Introvigne, and Hugh B. Urban. Rebecca Moore, another towering figure in the field, provided invaluable feedback to earlier drafts and wisely suggested the inclusion of glossaries.

Portions of this Element originally appeared in my article "Scientology Studies 2.0: Lessons Learned and Paths Forward," written during my postdoc at SDSU and published in *Religion Compass 14*(2) (2020). Section 3 is based on "Walking in Ron's Footsteps: 'Pilgrimage' Sites of the Church of Scientology" (*Numen*, *63*[1] [2016]). Appendix A expands on a timeline I first authored for Brill's *Handbook of Scientology* (2017), coedited by James R. Lewis and Kjersti Hellesøy.

I am grateful, as always, to Yvette Westbrook for feedback and proofreading. Finally, my thanks and love go to my wife, Rachel, for the large and small ways that we work together and make our own history. I dedicate this work to her and to our children, Noah and Dakota.

Cambridge Elements ≡

New Religious Movements

Series Editors

James R. Lewis

Wuhan University

James R. Lewis is Professor of Philosophy at Wuhan University, China. He currently edits or co-edits four book series, is the general editor for the *Alternative Spirituality and Religion Review* and the associate editor for the *Journal of Religion and Violence*. His publications include *The Cambridge Companion to Religion and Terrorism* (Cambridge University Press 2017) and *Falun Gong: Spiritual Warfare and Martyrdom* (Cambridge University Press 2018).

Rebecca Moore

San Diego State University

Rebecca Moore is Emerita Professor of Religious Studies at San Diego State University. She has written numerous books and articles on Peoples Temple and the Jonestown tragedy. Publications include *Beyond Brainwashing: Perspectives on Cultic Violence* (Cambridge University Press 2018) and *Peoples Temple and Jonestown in the Twenty-First Century* (Cambridge University Press 2022). She is reviews editor for *Nova Religio*, the quarterly journal on new and emergent religions published by University of California Press.

About the Series

Elements in New Religious Movements go beyond cult stereotypes and popular prejudices to present new religions and their adherents in a scholarly and engaging manner. Case studies of individual groups, such as Transcendental Meditation and Scientology, provide in-depth consideration of some of the most well known, and controversial, groups. Thematic examinations of women, children, science, technology, and other topics focus on specific issues unique to these groups. Historical analyses locate new religions in specific religious, social, political, and cultural contexts. These examinations demonstrate why some groups exist in tension with the wider society and why others live peaceably in the mainstream. The series demonstrates the differences, as well as the similarities, within this great variety of religious expressions. To discuss contributing to this series please contact Professor Moore.

Cambridge Elements ≡

New Religious Movements

Elements in the Series

The Sound Current Tradition: A Historical Overview
David Christopher Lane

Brainwashing: Reality or Myth?
Massimo Introvigne

L. Ron Hubbard and Scientology Studies
Donald A. Westbrook

A full series listing is available at: www.cambridge.org/ENRM